The Genealogist's
GOOGLE TOOLBOX

A Genealogist's Guide to the Most Powerful

Free Online Research Tools Available!

W9-AYP-828

Lisa Louise Cooke

Other books and DVDs by Lisa Louise Cooke are available at the Genealogy Gems website at http://www.GenealogyGems.com

Editor: Vienna Thomas
Assistant Editor: Lacey C. Cooke
Cover Design by Lisa Louise Cooke

Disclaimer:

To be clear, I am first and foremost a genealogy podcaster. My goal is to teach my listeners and readers innovative ways to use existing online tools specifically for their genealogy research. I have absolutely no affiliation with Google.

The Google tools discussed in this book are a group of constantly evolving programs. It's only natural that some of the websites and tools I refer to and points I mention in this book will change over time, which is out of my control. The good news is that you can tune in to the Genealogy Gems Podcast at www.GenealogyGems.com and get the latest news.

Also keep in mind that in this book we are not just covering step-by-step instructions but also overarching concepts. These concepts will serve you well even if websites or data are changed. And of course, you can always tap into the Help section of any tool for specific problem solving.

About the Author

Lisa Louise Cooke is the producer and host of *The Genealogy Gems Podcast*, and *Family History: Genealogy Made Easy* podcast. Both Internet audio shows are featured in iTunes and at www.genealogygems.com. She is a national conference speaker, author, podcast producer (*Family Tree Magazine Podcast*) and author of several articles and videos for *Family Tree Magazine*. A wife and mother of three grown daughters, she is devoted to helping families cultivate their place in history.

DEDICATION

To my husband Bill,
Whose belief in me never waivers,
Support of me never wanes,
And who selflessly let me have the spare bedroom for an office.
None of this is possible without you!

&

And to my first grandchild David William Cooke
You are the long awaited, perfect addition to our family tree!

TABLE OF CONTENTS

INTRODUCTION

Page 1

CHAPTER 1

Caffeine & Search Options Column - Page 5

CHAPTER 2

Basic & Advanced Search - Page 11

CHAPTER 3

Search Strategies for High-Quality Results - Page 21

CHAPTER 4

Site Search & Resurrecting Web Sites - Page 35

CHAPTER 5

Image Search - Page 41

CHAPTER 6

Google Alerts - Page 53

CHAPTER 7

Gmail – Page 59

CHAPTER 8

iGoogle – Your Personal Genealogy Homepage – Page 69

CHAPTER 9

Google Books – Page 87

CHAPTER 10

Google News Timeline – Page 99

CHAPTER 11

Google Translate & Translation Toolkit – Page 109

CHAPTER 12

YouTube and Google Video – Page 119

CHAPTER 13

Google Earth Overview – Page 131

CHAPTER 14

Google Earth – Ancestral Homes and Locations – Page 147

CHAPTER 15

Google Earth – Organizing, Naming, and Sharing – Page 153

CHAPTER 16

Google Earth – Historic Maps and Images – Page 161

CHAPTER 17

Google Earth – Plotting Your Ancestor's Homestead – Page 175

CHAPTER 18

Google Earth – Fun with Images and Video – Page 183

CHAPTER 19

Family History Tour Maps – Page 195

APPENDIX

Find it Quick: The "How To" Index – Page 200

INTRODUCTION
Get Ready to Build Your Family Tree
Faster and Sturdier

At least as far back as 1907 the advertising slogan of Cleveland, Ohio's American Fork & Hoe Co. "True Temper" tool line was:

THE RIGHT TOOL FOR THE RIGHT JOB.

Company executives knew that it was important to farmers to save time, labor, and money, and their advertising leaflets made a clear case as to how tools made for the job at hand could do just that.

When it comes to your online genealogical research, you also need the top of the line tools to help you get the job done. In this book you will learn how to fill your genealogy toolbox with free state-of-the-art online tools that are built to search, translate, message, and span the globe. In order to get the right tools for the job, we're heading outside the genealogy community, and to the folks who dominate the online world: Google.

Introduction to Google

The big white empty screen of the classic Google webpage < www.google.com > is quite ironic considering the vast amount of free tools offered by Google and the power of their monumental search engine. So while you have a handle on the basics of search, it's time to take your research to the next level. We will cover a wide range of advanced techniques and tools that will help you get the most from this quiet giant.

Know Your History

In order to really be able to maximize the power of Google search, it's important to understand what goes on behind that search box and big white webpage.

Let's start by refreshing our understanding how Google search works by watching the video *How Search Works* by Google.

VIDEO: How Search Works
http://www.youtube.com/watch?v=BNHR6IQJGZs

Search Strategies For High-Quality Results

It's time to put an end to fruitless Google searches.

What do I mean by fruitless searches? Searches that:
- bring up thousands (if not hundreds of thousands!) of results
- contain websites on topics totally unrelated to your search
- include websites containing completely unreliable information.

In this chapter we are going to tackle these challenges by looking at why these fruitless searches occur and how to correct the situation so we can obtain higher quality results.

Why Fruitless Searches Occur

One of the primary reasons why researchers end up with searches full of countless low-quality results is that they fail to recognize two fundamentals about Google search:

1. Search is an art not an exact science
2. High quality search results are not the product of single searches, but a process

In other words, there is no one answer for effective searches. Rather, it's critical to understand the tools at your disposal and how to use them in sequence to achieve the desired results.

The primary tools available to the searcher include:

- Advanced Search Strategies
- Search Operators
- Basic Search
- The Search Options Column

Mixing and matching these tools in a variety of ways (as the particular search scenario requires) is really an art. Much like the painter mixes colors over and over until the desired hue is achieved, advanced Googlers blend the tools together in a variety of ways until quality results are achieved. Rarely do the best results come from one search attempt. This is particularly true in genealogical search because there are so many factors involved when it comes to searching for our complex ancestors.

Google's New Search Index: Caffeine

In early June 2010 Google announced the completion of a new web indexing system called Caffeine. According to the folks at Google, "Caffeine provides 50 percent fresher results for web searches than our last index, and it's the largest collection of web content we've offered…you can now find links to relevant content much sooner after it is published than was possible ever before." Considering the speed with which content is being added to the Web and the wider variety of content (videos, blogs, images, etc.) available, this should prove to be a big bonus.

The old index was made up of layers that revisited websites and refreshed the Google index at different rates. The top layer refreshed every couple of weeks, while the bottom layer had a fairly significant delay.

Caffeine, on the other hand, analyzes smaller chunks of the Web constantly and adds them to the index right away. This method should provide a more consistently updated Google index and faster access to you as the end user.

One of the areas where you may see an improvement is in your genealogical Google Alerts (which we will cover in more detail later in this book). Since Google is delivering a fresher index more quickly, Google Alerts should be able to deliver the searches you have set up to your email inbox more quickly.

Finally, to put Caffeine's ability to index web pages into perspective, consider Google's description of its enormous scale: "Every second Caffeine processes hundreds of thousands of pages in parallel. If this were a pile of paper it would grow three miles taller every second. Caffeine takes up nearly 100 million gigabytes of storage in one database and adds new information at a rate of hundreds of thousands of gigabytes per day. You would need 625,000 of the largest iPods to store that much information; if these were stacked end-to-end they would go for more than 40 miles."

Google's goal was to have Caffeine be a "robust foundation" that makes it possible for them to build an even faster and more comprehensive search engine. They also wanted a search engine that can grow as the Internet grows while still delivering the most relative searches possible. This goal implies that we will want to keep our eye on Google because even more improvements are on the horizon.

CHAPTER 1
Search Options Column

The first thing to keep in mind is that when you search with Google, you are not searching the live Web. At first glance this may sound like a negative, but answer this question: When you find a very large genealogy reference book at the library, would it be more effective and efficient to thumb through the hundreds of pages in the book, or flip to the back of the book and look through the index for what you need?

In addition to the new Caffeine indexing system, Google has made changes to the Google search results page that will put more tools at your fingertips.

The new Search Options Column (above) is dedicated to helping you quickly refine your search. While many of the options aren't necessarily brand new, they are more accessible now.

Obviously Google isn't designing its tools and features with genealogists in mind. Their primary business is ad sales. However, the following video is still worth viewing because it provides a quick overview of the Search Options Column and how it works.

VIDEO: *Google Search Options*
http://www.youtube.com/watch?v=MtirDMfcOKE&feature=channel_page

Here's what the new Search Options Column can do for your research

When we enter into a new phase of our research we often need to get our bearings by evaluating what's available online as well as learn more about the nature of the records we are looking for and their place in history. In this example, let's say that we want to learn more about Immigration and specifically Ellis Island passenger lists. Here's how the results page will look when we click the SEARCH button:

Notice the Search Option Column on the left side of the page. As indicated in the column, our current search results (all 157,000) cover all areas of the web – "Everything." To reveal more options, click the down arrow next to the word MORE. A wider range of search options than ever before are now a click away.

Images

One of those options is Image Search. The Images option isn't new, but remains one of the most powerful and underutilized options in Google. Why is it so powerful? Because you can quickly assess which of the websites in your results list actually contains digitized passenger lists, those that have photos, and so on. Depending on what you are looking for, a visual search can really speed up the process.

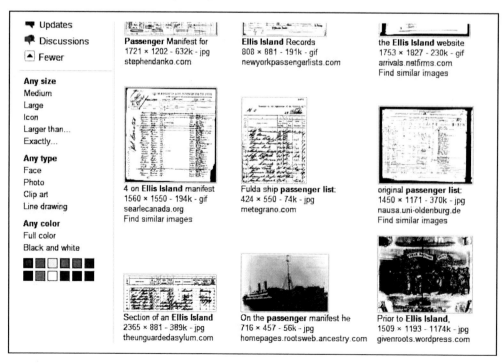

Clicking the MORE button now gives you control over finding a certain type of image. You can search by size or color, which can be very helpful if you are looking for something specific to match a project you are working on. Under the heading of ANY TYPE you will find tools that will really zero in on images of:

- Faces
- Photos
- Clip Art
- Line Drawings

If you are looking for maps associated with immigration through Ellis Island, you can quickly weed out portraits and photographs by clicking on LINE DRAWING.

When you find a map in the Line Drawing Results, click the "Find Similar Images" link beneath it and you will have a myriad of maps:

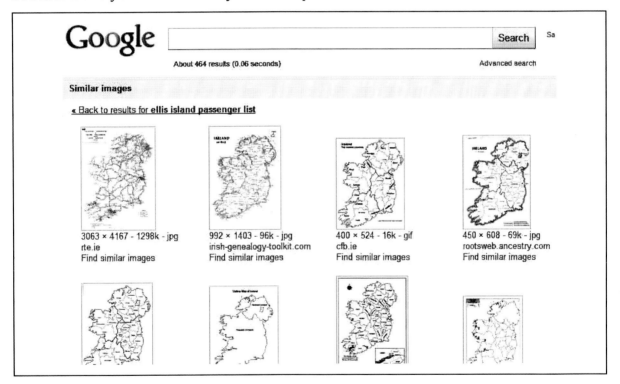

Video

Also in the Search Option Column under MORE is VIDEO SEARCH, where you'll find everything - movie trailers, historic film footage, other genealogists' trips to Ellis Island, first-hand accounts by Ellis Island immigrants, and more. (*Image Right*) Video is a fascinating way to add historic context to your research and even connect with others who may be interested in the same research areas.

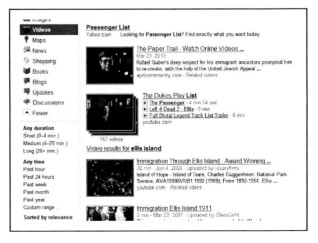

Maps

Planning a trip to Ellis Island? Click on the Map link and you'll have tons of useful information at your fingertips.

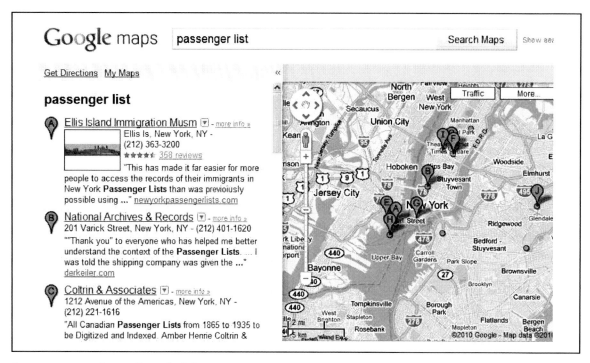

Learn more about Google Maps...
VIDEO: *How to Create a My Map in Google Maps*
http://www.youtube.com/watch?v=TftFnot5uXw

Blogs

And don't overlook the Blogs link. Genealogists all over the world are blogging about their research, ancestors, and genealogical interests. Click Blogs and discover a world of information not found anywhere else!

Expanding Your Horizons

If you would like to learn how to blog about your family history watch the four part video series "How to Blog Your Family History" at the Genealogy Gems YouTube Channel: http://www.youtube.com/GenealogyGems

Books

The vast collection at Google Books is just one click away with the BOOKS link:
VIDEO: *Searching for Your Ancestral Roots (with Google Books)*
http://www.youtube.com/watch?v=UwnbCmVrISQ

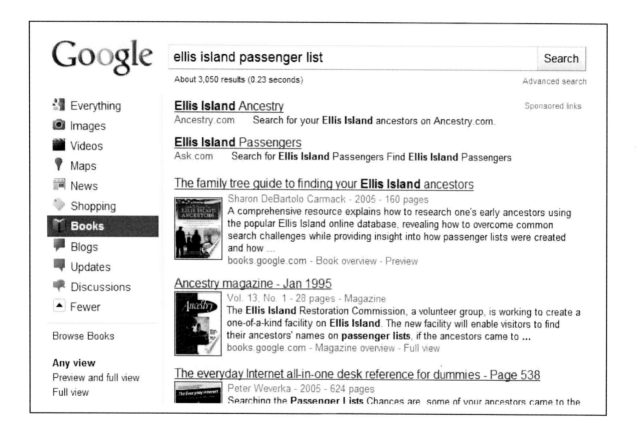

Exploring Your Options

As you click each of the options in the Search Options Column, note that a range of new options appear beneath the divider line. These are additional tools for refining your search and homing in on your target. In the case of BOOKS, these tools are much the same options you would find on the advanced search page, saving you time and effort.

Switching Up Your View

When you conduct a search you view the results in Standard View. However, there are a couple of additional options available to you that can give you a fresh perspective

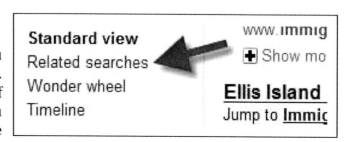

on your search.

Related Searches

Sometimes you aren't exactly sure what you are looking for or don't realize that there are other related website that might be of interest in your research. This is where RELATED SEARCHES comes in. A click of the Related Searches link in the Search Options Column will provide Google's best guess at searches that are closely related to your query that you may also find useful.

www.GenealogyGems.com

CHAPTER 2
Basic Search

Harness the Power of Google Search

Understanding core Google search techniques can take you a long way in your research. Once you master the basics, you can then add additional strategies that will help with your specific avenue of research.

There are two things you need to keep in mind as you conduct Internet searches:

1. What you want may not be out there – No matter how good the search strategies are, Google can't find what's not on the web.

2. The web is changing moment by moment. What isn't there now could be posted five minutes from now.

Basic Search Strategies

STRATEGY: Keep it Simple

Even though there are some great advanced search techniques, they won't apply to all of your searches. In fact, according to Google, advanced strategies are generally only needed about 5% of the time. The percentage may be higher for us as researchers because we are trying to locate specific information about our ancestors and we want to discern between people with the same names. However, the "Keep it Simple" principle usually applies. Google is designed to be most effective with simple, concise search queries. If you're looking for a particular business that your ancestor worked for, just enter the name, or as much of the name as you know. If you're looking for a particular concept, place, or product, start with the name.

If you're looking for a county court house, simply enter county courthouse and the name of the county or the zip code. Most queries do not require advanced operators or unusual syntax. Simple is definitely a good way to start.

Here are some simple guidelines to remember as you search:

1. In a search, every word matters! In general all the words you put in the query will be used, with a few exceptions.

2. Search is never case sensitive. It doesn't matter whether you type "los angeles" or "Los Angeles." Go ahead and save the time it takes to shift and stick to lower case.

3. Punctuation is generally ignored by Google search. This means you can't search on special characters such as @#$%^&*()=+[]\ .

STRATEGY: Imagine It and You Will Find It

As a genealogist you can probably imagine how another genealogist might record data about your ancestor on a web page. That's a big advantage when it comes to search. A search engine isn't human - all it can do is match words in your query with words on a page. Genealogists tend to use certain words when recording genealogical data and those are what you should be including in your query.

For example, a non-genealogist might type in a search box:

What is the birthday of George Washington Carver?

"Birthday" is not the term a genealogist or a records site would likely use on their web page. Using that word would probably bring up all kinds of pages that really aren't the type of genealogical data you are looking for.

Instead, as a genealogist you might want to use the following search:

George Washington Carver born died
or
George Washington Carver birth death

Again the strategy here is to use the kind of words that the author of the kind of page you would be interested in would use.

STRATEGY: Use Descriptive Words

The more targeted and unique the words are that you use in your query, the better results you will receive. Words like 'document,' 'info,' and 'website' are generally unnecessary. Again, the idea is to think like the person who has the information that you want on their website. Ask yourself: "What words would they use?"

Rather than searching:

What does the number next to the occupation code mean in the census?

Which results in nearly 1.5 million haphazard results, try:

Column 26D 1930 census meaning

This delivers around 3,400 results and the first 10 look like they will most certainly be able to answer the question. (Below)

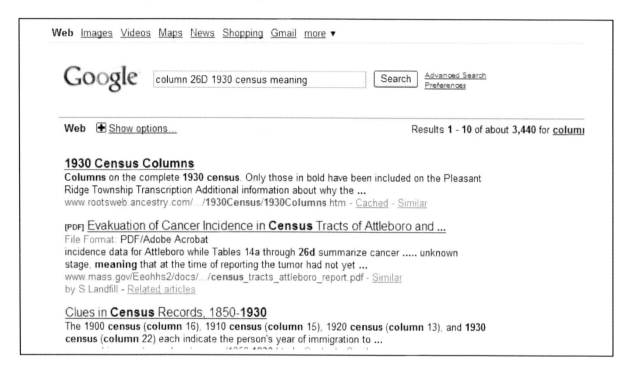

STRATEGY: Pull It All Together – Simple, Imagined, and Descriptive Searches

Keep it simple by using as few words and terms as possible. Each word you choose to add to your query should focus the query even more. Keeping it simple also means not focusing yourself out of results because your query has become too narrow. Since Google uses the words you search on, each additional word you add to your query will further limit the results.

That's where "imagining" comes in. Search is not an exact science because there's no way to really know what might be out there that would be helpful to your research. Simplicity leaves room for the gems you might not have realized could be out there on the Web.

STRATEGY: Use Multiple Searches

A good search is rarely done in one click of the Search button. Start by using a limited number of search words, and then add to it to focus in on what you want. If a particular word seems to not be hitting the mark, try another one.

You might want to start with a search such as:

Harold Carter birth Springfield

When the results indicate there are dozens of "Springfields" around the country, you would then add:

Harold Carter birth Springfield Ohio

Incorporating Operators

Searches are conducted with "search operators," which are terms that can help you further narrow or broaden your search. You may already be familiar with the common Boolean search operators AND, OR, NOT.

> ***VOCAB***: ***Boolean operator -*** a logical operator (or command) used in a system of logic developed by the English mathematician George Boole. There are 3 Boolean operators: AND, OR, NOT.

Here are some examples of how Boolean operators can make a difference in the quality of your searches.

Let's say that you are searching a Harold Carter from Springfield, Ohio and there happens to be a prominent man named Harold Carter from Springfield, Missouri who keeps popping up in your search results. By using the Boolean operator "NOT" you can sweep Mr. Carter from Missouri out of the way and off your results page:

First search: *Harold Carter birth Springfield Ohio*

Revised search: *Harold Carter birth Springfield Ohio NOT Missouri*

Here's another example. If you are researching an uncle who played sax in a blues band and you'd like to learn more about that part of his life you might incorporate the Boolean operator AND this way:

George Crandall blues AND jazz

Notice I didn't include the word "band" in this initial search. Why force Google to only provide pages that include that word? If the words *jazz* or *blues* appear on a page that also includes *George Crandall*, chances are you'll be in the right spot. There's also a good chance that the person who published the web page you want refers to George's band as a "group" or a "trio." Using a generic word like "band" could have a negative effect on your results.

Here's a third example. You may not be sure whether Great Grandmother Smith is buried in Manhattan or Brooklyn. Here's how to search for cemeteries in either city:

Cemeteries Manhattan OR Brooklyn

Advanced Search

After you've exhausted the basic search techniques, it's time to shift into high gear with Advanced Search. This will help you search with more precision and hopefully achieve even better results. Here are some great advanced techniques to try:

"+" Search

Google ignores common words and characters such as *where, the, how*, and other digits and letters which slow down your search without improving the results. However, if a common word is essential to getting the results you are looking for, you can include it by putting a space and then a "+" sign in front of it.

Here's how to add the digits "III" in a search for John Smith III:

John Smith +III

Quotations Marks

When you want to find an exact phrase in a web site, enclose the phrase in quotation marks. For example:

"U.S. Federal Census"

This will bring up websites with that exact phrase and no variation.

Alternative to NOT

A quicker way to eliminate a particular word from your search results list, rather than typing the word NOT before the word in the search box, is to type a minus sign and the word. For example, you might be searching for the surname Lincoln but you don't want to get inundated with results for Abraham Lincoln. You could search on:

Lincoln –Abraham

The word *Lincoln* but NOT the word *Abraham* will be returned in your search results. This works great for eliminating a word that is commonly linked to your search term but has no bearing on your research.

Quick Definition Search

Have you ever come across a term in your research and you were unsure of its meaning? For example, you see the word cooper in the occupation column of the census but don't recall what a cooper does. Simply type the following in the search box:

define:cooper

With one click of the Search button you'll have the answer: *a craftsman who makes or repairs wooden barrels or tubs.*

```
Web  Images  Videos  Maps  News  Shopping  Gmail  more ▼

Google    define:cooper                          Search    Advanced Search
                                                           Preferences

Web

Related phrases:  john cooper  william cooper  gary cooper  david cooper  chris cooper  ashley cooper  r
cooper

Definitions of cooper on the Web:

  • United States industrialist who built the first American locomotive; founded Cooper Union in New York
  • United States film actor noted for his portrayals of strong silent heroes (1901-1961)
  • United States novelist noted for his stories of American Indians and the frontier life (1789-1851)
  • make barrels and casks
  • a craftsman who makes or repairs wooden barrels or tubs
    wordnetweb.princeton.edu/perl/webwn

  • This is a list of characters in the American animated television series Ben 10 and its sequel ™. This lis
    than one episode.
    en.wikipedia.org/wiki/Cooper_(Ben_10)
```

Words Apart Search

Sometimes the words that you are looking for won't appear next to each other even though they normally do. For example, you may be looking for a city directory and normally you would expect to see the two words together as a phrase: *city directory*.

However, by using an asterisk to set them apart, you may find the perfect result that searching for them together or with quotation marks around them may have missed.

*City * directory*

Results could include:
  • *City phone directory*
  • *City telephone directory*
  • *City and county directory*, etc.

Synonym Search

If you want to search not only for your search term but also for its synonyms, place the tilde sign (~) immediately in front of your search term.

For example, to learn more about an industry your ancestor was involved in such as the railroad, you can search for train history and railroad information like this:

~train ~history

This would then give you:
  • *railroad history*
  • *railroad past*, etc.

```
Web  Images  Videos  Maps  News  Shopping  Gmail  more ▼

Google    ~train ~history                          Search   Advanced Search
                                                            Preferences

Web  ⊞ Show options...                                      Results 1 - 10

Railroad Invention and History
History of railroad locomotive and train innovations - past - present - future.
inventors.about.com/library/inventors/blrailroad.htm - Cached - Similar

History - Official SUBWAY Restaurants' Web Site
www.subway.com/subwayroot/AboutSubway/history/subwayHistory.aspx - Similar

Amtrak - Wikipedia, the free encyclopedia
1 History. 1.1 Passenger rail service before Amtrak; 1.2 Causes of decline of passenger rail.
1.2.1 Government regulation and labor issues. 2 Taxation ...
History - Taxation - Public funding - Labor issues
en.wikipedia.org/wiki/Amtrak - Cached - Similar
```

Another Example:

cooke ~genealogy

This would not only bring up sites that include 'cooke and genealogy," but also "cooke and family tree," "cooke and family history," and even "cooke and surname."

Numrange Search
A Numrange search delivers results containing numbers in a given range. Just type in two numbers, separated by two periods with no spaces, into the search box along with your search terms. This would be an ideal search if you were unsure of an exact year. For example:

George Crandall 1850..1860

Link Search
Let's say that you find a terrific genealogy website all about your specific family line. Wouldn't it be nice to know who else out there on the Web is interested in that family line too?

By doing a search using the search term *link:* you will get a list of web pages that have links to that web site. For instance, if you found a great website about your saxophone-playing uncle on the *Crandall Family Web Site*, you could try the following search:

link:www.crandallfamilywebsite.com

Note there can be no space between the "link:" and the web page url.

Related Search

Similar to the Link Search, the Related Search will list web sites that are "similar" to a specified web site. The following search will list web sites that are similar to the *Crandall Family Website*:

related:www.crandallfamilywebsite.com

Note there can be no space between the "related:" and the web page url.

Allintitle Search

If you start a search with *allintitle:* Google will restrict the results to only pages that have all of the search words in the title. For example, to get only documents which contain *Minnesota, railroad,* and *history* in the title:

Allintitle: Minnesota railroad history

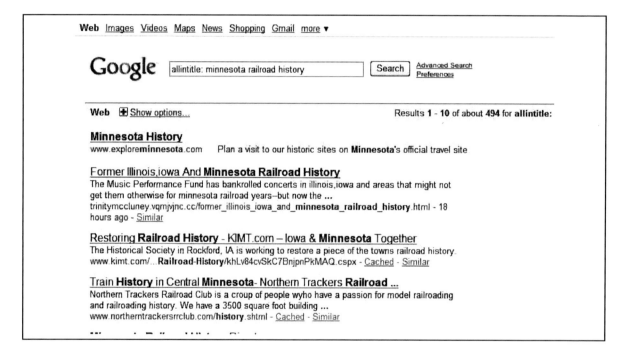

Allinurl: Search

Have you ever tried to remember a website address for a great genealogy website and although you couldn't remember the exact address, you recalled some of the keywords? If you start a search with *allinurl:* Google will restrict your search results to only those that have all of the search words in the URL address.

For example, if an ancestor worked for the Oregon Pacific railroad and you knew that the words Oregon and Pacific were in the URL address, you could do a search on:

Allinurl: Oregon Pacific

And the results page would include the Oregon Pacific Railroad Company web site at http://www.oregonpacificrr.com/

Note: punctuation will be ignored in this type of search. *Oregon/Pacific* will ignore the slash and give you the same result as no slash at all.

If You're In A Hurry...

If these techniques seem like a challenge to remember or you're in a hurry, try Google's Advanced Search page. You'll find the Advanced Search link next to the search box on the Google home page. You can also get there directly by going to: http://www.google.com/advanced_search.

At the Advanced Search page you will find additional search options:

Language: Specify in which language you'd like your results.

Date: Restrict your results to the past 3, 6, or 12-month periods.

SafeSearch: Eliminates adult sites from search results.

Keys to Success

Key Concept: Keep it Simple
Less is more when it comes to search. Start simple and then revise your search to follow the right path.

Key Concept: Use Your Imagination
Think like someone who would post a web page with the kind of information you want. Think like a genealogist for charts and reports, think like a railroad historian for background information on the railroad your grandfather worked for, and think like a librarian when searching for books.

Key Concept: Use Focused, Descriptive Words
The bottom line: each word should pack a search punch!

Key Concept: Try a Variety of Search Options
Remember: "search strategies" is a plural phrase and implies that a number of searches need to be conducted to get the best results.

Key Concept: Don't Stop At a Great Website
When you find a helpful web site, before you leave you have two more searches to do:

Relatedto: Search
Link: Search

These two searches may reveal another great web site you might have missed on the same topic.

CHAPTER 3
Put An End To Fruitless Google Searches

The Process of Advanced Search

The best way to illustrate the process of incorporating advanced search strategies is through a search case study that tackles the most common challenges.

Challenge #1: Too Many Low-Quality Results

Search Goal: Locate enumeration district maps for Sibley County, Minnesota for the available census years.

Here's the typical keyword-packed search:

Search #1: ENUMERATION DISTRICT MAP SIBLEY COUNTY
Results: 6,080

There are far too many results to cope with. One of the problems with such a search is that Google is looking for web page that includes any combination of the keywords. Several refer to a person with the last name "Sibley" in a "county" in another state! This is where operators come in to play. We need Google to only search for "Sibley county" rather than "Sibley" and "County" randomly on the page. To do this we use our first tool: quotation marks.

Search #2: ENUMERATION DISTRICT MAP "SIBLEY COUNTY"
Results: 1,680

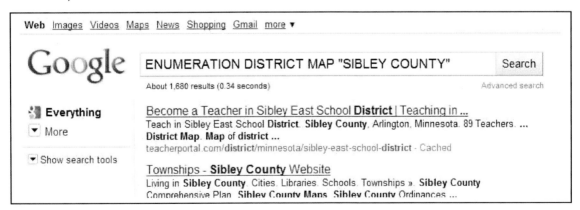

These simple quotation marks alone eliminated 4,400 results that were not specifically for Sibley County! It is a vast improvement, but just the beginning. Since we are in search of an "enumeration district" map and not just any mention of "enumeration" and "district," our next step is to apply quotation marks to those key words.

Search #3: "ENUMERATION DISTRICT" MAP "SIBLEY COUNTY"

Results: 42

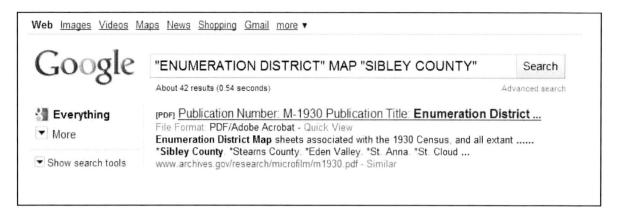

Again, this is a great improvement. Look at the first result listed. As you can see, the quality of the results is increasing dramatically. The description of this web page starts with "Enumeration District Map." So why didn't we put quotation marks around "ENUMERATION DISTRICT MAP" in our search? We can answer that question with a question: What if the web page said, "Here is a map of the state of Minnesota Enumeration Districts"? That result would not have appeared, and yet may have been of great value. This is where the "art" comes in. Be a Search Artist by keeping these two things in mind:

- Think like a web page writer
"Enumeration District" is a recognized phrase in genealogy and the webpage writer who is specifically talking about enumeration district maps is highly likely to use it. However, simply including the word MAP will remove all the pages that never mention maps and therefore is effective on its own. Including MAP within the quotation marks needlessly restricts pages where the writer does not use that exact phrase.

- Keep searches as simple as possible while fine-tuning each search attempt
Again, we can go back to our painter analogy. The painter adds just enough tint to achieve the result and avoid muddying the overall color. We don't want to muddy the waters of search with needless restrictions. Each tool employed restricts results and we don't want to miss a valuable web page. To see this in action, give it a try:

Search #4: "ENUMERATION DISTRICT MAP" "SIBLEY COUNTY"
Results: 1

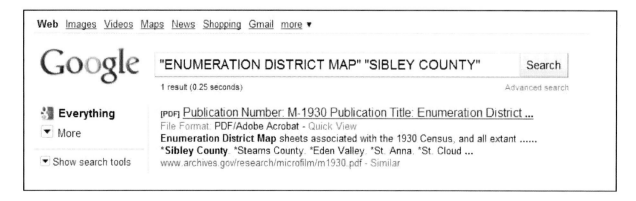

One result is not enough to feel confident you got the best result. This is proof that simple is better. Let's stick with Search #3, which includes a manageable number of results: 42.

While we could take the time to go through all 42 results, that would still be very time consuming. At this point take a moment and look over the descriptions of the types of web pages we are retrieving. We still see sites that may not be quite what we are looking for. The process continues. Let's use one of the primary tools, the Search Options Column.

By clicking the Images link in the upper left corner of the page, Google will run the same search, but for images rather than text webpages.

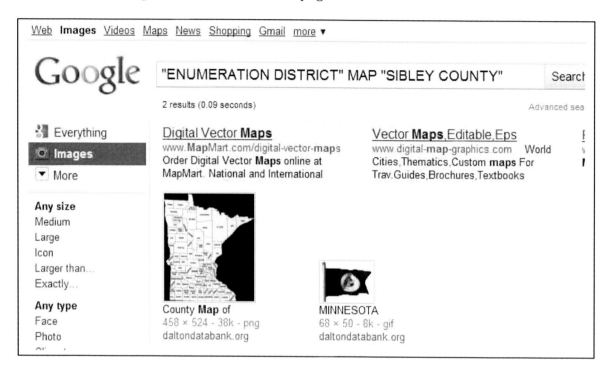

The results are meager – just two. This tells us something very important about what is likely not available on the Internet. Digitized maps of Sibley County enumeration districts will likely not be found online. So what we are probably going to find are repositories of such maps, which is the next best thing.

To get back to our original search, click the Web link in the upper left corner.

Let's stop again and think like a web page publisher. Because enumeration districts are not limited to historic census records and we are only interested in maps for the available historic enumerations, there is still more whittling down that can be done on these results through continuing the search process.

We know that currently the most recent available enumeration is 1930. Let's try adding "1930" to the search to see if we can find a reference to an enumeration map for that past census.

Search #5: "ENUMERATION DISTRICT" MAP "SIBLEY COUNTY" 1930
Results: 32

Of all of the result descriptions, the first result looks like the closest match. It's from the National Archives and refers specifically to "Enumeration District Map Sheets" associated with the 1930 census and "Sibley County."

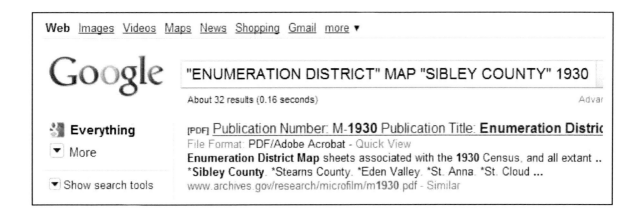

It is not a big surprise that the National Archives would be a source for such maps, but had there been another repository chances are it would be near the top of the list. With just 32 results, looking through each would not be too burdensome. And again, some could be skipped all together simply from the description provided in the result.

Publication Number: M-1930

Publication Title: Enumeration District Maps for the Fifteenth Census of the United States, 1930

Date Published: 2001

ENUMERATION DISTRICT MAPS FOR THE FIFTEENTH CENSUS
OF THE UNITED STATES, 1930

Introduction

On the 36 rolls of this microfilm publication, M1930, are reproduced the Enumeration District Maps for the Fifteenth Census of the United States, 1930. These maps number some 8,345 separate sheets and they are part of the Records of the Bureau of the Census, Record Group 29. They are housed at the National Archives and Records Administration Building in College Park, Maryland.

Background

An enumeration district, as used by the Bureau of the Census, was an area that could be covered by a single enumerator (census taker) in one census period (2-4 weeks for the 1930 Census). Enumeration districts varied in size from several city blocks in densely populated urban areas to an entire county in sparsely populated rural areas. Census jurisdictions, divisions, districts, or subdivisions were used in earlier censuses and the terms "enumeration district" and "enumerator" were first used in the 1880 Census.

By clicking on the link we are taken to a PDF (above), and it looks like we've hit pay dirt!

In the first paragraph we learn that the National Archives has 36 rolls of microfilmed enumeration district maps in their collection housed at the National Archives and Records Administration Building in College Park, Maryland. The next paragraph answers the question as to which census schedules have enumeration district maps: "Census jurisdictions, divisions, districts, or subdivisions were used in earlier censuses and the terms "enumeration district" and "enumerator" were first used in the 1880 census." Now we know that if we want to locate maps earlier than 1880 we need to change the keywords we use to find them.

As illustrated in this section, it is clear that the art of search is a series of steps, with each step based on the knowledge gained in the previous one taken.

QUICK TIPS

You can dig deeper into a high quality search result such as the National Archives web page we discovered in our search by using a couple of quick tricks:

QUICK TIP #1: How to Alter the URL Address to Find More in Sub Directories
- Click your mouse at the end of the URL address of the current page

- Backspace to remove "1930.pdf" and replace it with "1920.pdf" (or the year you are looking for)
- Press ENTER on your keyboard

If there is a similar document available for that census year and the Webmaster has uniformly created the pages, you might get lucky and very quickly get what you are looking for.

In this case we receive a page explaining that the site has been redesigned and how to locate further information. However, this trick is worth a try since it is quick and easy to do.

QUICK TIP #2: How to Take A Web Page Back To Its Roots
By removing subdirectories from the URL address you can quickly be taken to the main homepage for the site where you can often find the site's menu and a search box.

- Start with the page of interest that you found in your results
- Click your mouse at the end of the URL address
- Backspace to remove the portion of the address that appears after ".gov" or ".com"
- Press ENTER

Above Image: By removing the subdirectory "microfilm" and the 1930.pdf you are now in the Research area of the website where you can focus your search. (Sure enough there is a link on this page to Genealogy and a search box.)

Challenge #2: Surnames That Double as Common Words or Are Shared By Famous People

Few families escape the dilemma of surnames that also double as common words in the

English language. Here are just a few examples:

Barber	Best	Bishop
Booth	Church	Coffin
Free	Lemon	West

Thankfully there are ways to refine your search to bypass the non-genealogical results clutter.

Let's take a look at the Free family of Cleveland, Ohio. In the 1930 census, Carl is a 53 year-old motorman for the Railroad in Cleveland, Ohio, and a military veteran. In this example let's look for a death record for Carl online and start with the obvious keywords.

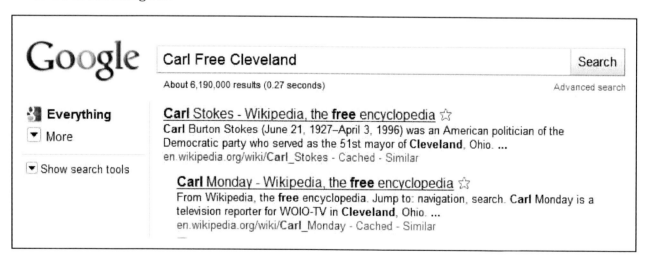

Search #1: CARL FREE CLEVELAND
Results: 6,190,000!! And the first two refer to the "free" Wikipedia website! Not exactly what we are looking for.

In an effort to dramatically narrow down the field, let's focus on Carl's obituary. By adding a plus sign directly in front of the keyword OBITUARY we are telling Google the results page must include the word obituary.

Search #2: CARL FREE CLEVELAND +OBITUARY
Results: 194,000
As you can see in these results we are still plagued by Wikipedia results. So those need to be eliminated. We will do that by adding "-Wikipedia".

Search #3: CARL FREE CLEVELAND +OBITUARY –WIKIPEDIA
Results: 159,000

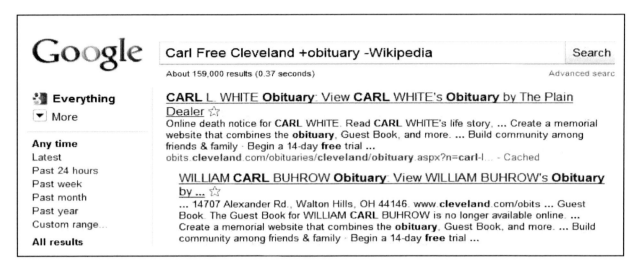

Thinking like an obituary writer, another keyword that will appear in Carl's obituary would be the name of his wife: Catherine.

Search #4: CARL FREE CLEVELAND +OBITUARY –WIKIPEDIA +CATHERINE
Results: 58,600

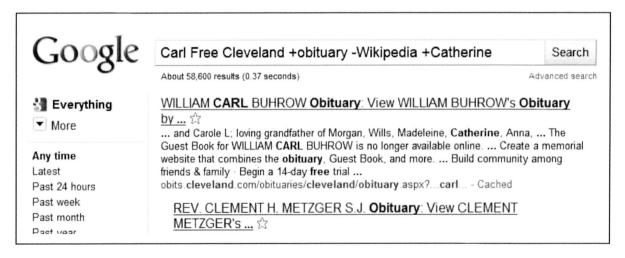

We've come a long way from over 6 million results to now be in the thousands range. But there is still more fine-tuning to do. Let's apply the same logic as the previous search and add the name of Carl and Catherine's oldest child, Walter.

Search #5: CARL FREE CLEVELAND +OBITUARY –WIKIPEDIA +CATHERINE +WALTER
Results: 19,000

As we see the effectiveness of adding key family names to the search, we need to keep an eye on the terms we have already employed. Keep in mind the principle of keeping the search as simple as possible to avoid eliminating a high-quality result, while using enough tools to get to what we are looking for. In this case, the word OBITUARY may be more of a hindrance than help. While we are indeed looking for an obituary and the word will likely appear on a genealogy website, not every obituary that appears in the newspaper includes that exact word. Since search is an art form, there's no harm in testing this theory by removing the word obituary from our query.

<u>Search #6: CARL FREE CLEVELAND –WIKIPEDIA +CATHERINE +WALTER</u>
Results: 265,000

265,000 results is a significantly high number, so for now we will retain +OBITUARY, but keep the option of removing it for later use when we have further fine-tuned the search.

As we scroll through the results we start to get a better idea of which words associated with FREE are reducing the quality of results. Here are some phrases that stand out:

- Free Lookup
- Free Man
- For Free
- Free Information
- Free of Charge

The good news is that we can eliminate as many words as we wish. There's no limit to the length of your search criteria. In this case it would probably be safe to eliminate CHARGE and LOOKUP. Play around with your options but be careful not to remove a word that could appear in a death notice or obituary (ex. MAN, INFORMATION).

Again, thinking like a writer of obituaries, let's try altering +CATHERINE to +"wife Catherine" a phrase commonly found in obituaries.

<u>Search #7: CARL FREE CLEVELAND –WIKIPEDIA +"WIFE CATHERINE" +WALTER</u>
Results: 3,200

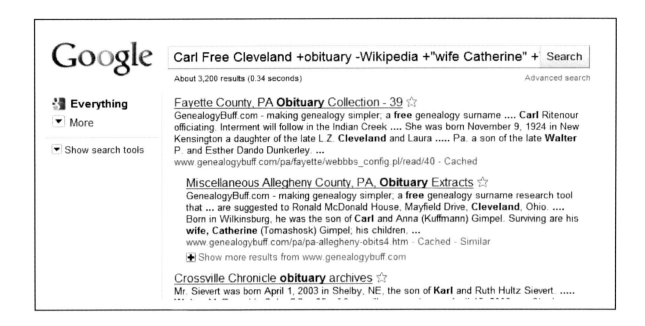

A significant improvement because not only are we down to 3,200 results, but the quality of the results has also increased dramatically. All of the results on the first page of results are obituaries!

Since that approach worked so well, let's try it with Carl's son, Walter. We are safe in doing so because the census record tells us that Carl has one "son."

Search #8: CARL FREE CLEVELAND –WIKIPEDIA +"WIFE CATHERINE" +"SON WALTER"
Results: 504

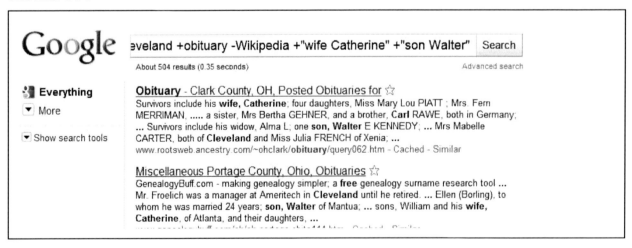

This approach achieved the desired results!
Let's take another hard look at the current search criteria:
CARL FREE CLEVELAND –WIKIPEDIA +"WIFE CATHERINE" +"SON WALTER"

So far we haven't manipulated Carl's name. We could put quotation marks around "CARL FREE" but that would eliminate any mention of Carl that includes a middle initial or middle name. Another option would be to add quotation marks and an asterisk between

CARL and FREE to serve as a wildcard holding the place of a possible middle name. However this can be ineffective when it comes to surnames that have a double meaning as a common word. The asterisk makes room for one *or more* words between the first and last name, which leaves a lot of room for the common English meaning of the surname to creep back in. Here's an example:

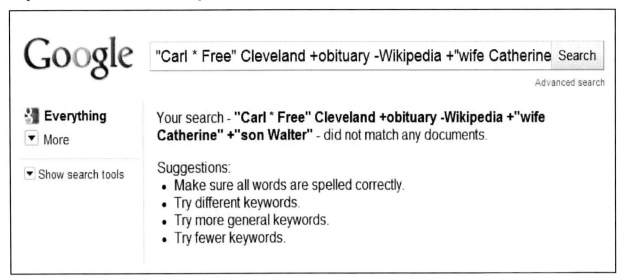

As you can see that brings the results to zero. However, note the "Suggestions" that Google makes for improving search results:

- Make sure all words are spelled correctly
- Try different Keywords
- Try more general keywords
- Try fewer keywords

In this case a quick try of fewer keywords and operators is warranted. (See Below)

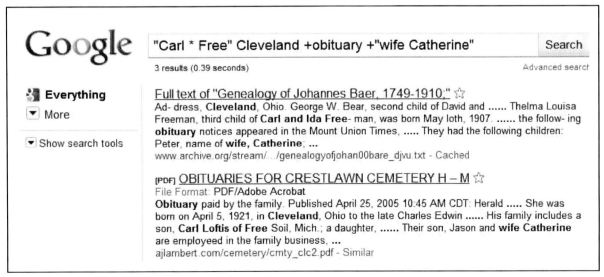

QUICK TIP: Leave a Bread Crumb Trail
As you can see, challenging searches can take many revisions, and just as with documenting your sources, it is very important to document the search attempts you've made. As you mix and match keywords and operators, keep track of which steer you closest to the types of results you desire. A simple spreadsheet or table in a word processing document can do the trick.

Search Summary

In the case of Carl Free of Cleveland, Ohio it's safe to say at this point that an obituary is not available on a non-subscription web page. While it may have been more satisfying to use an example of a search that results in the happy ending of a digitized obituary, the truth is that is often not the case. However, new content is constantly being added to the Web and Google's new Caffeine is finding it faster than ever. So our next step is to select one or more of the most promising search scenarios and set them up as Google Alerts at http://www.google.com/alerts, which we will cover in Chapter 7.

Further Learning:
VIDEO: *Google Alerts Genealogy Style by genealogyscrounge*
http://www.youtube.com/watch?v=zckI0SgOTp8

More Challenges, More Strategies

Sometimes adding the word GENEALOGY will aid in narrowing your search, but it depends on the surname. The surname WARD can deliver results having to do with "hospital ward," and "voting ward," but the addition of GENEALOGY tends to weed those out. Just beware, the word GENEALOGY might do more harm than good in a search for the FREE family!

In addition to surnames that double as common words in the English language, there are also those problematic surnames that are shared by very famous people that populate your results. If you are researching the surname Lincoln, Bush, or other prominent name then you've probably already experienced this challenge.

Use operators such as the minus sign to remove unwanted terms that apply to the famous person but not to your family.

Simple examples include:

John Lincoln -Abraham

Bush Family –president

Finally, if you are interested in only serious scholarly work on a particular topic or family you can restrict your search to courts, universities, academic publishers, and other scholarly content providers with Google Scholar.

Go to http://scholar.google.com

In the case of both Google Scholar and Google.com, the Advanced Search page can be accessed by clicking the link next to the SEARCH button. Using Advanced Scholar Search saves you from having to remember all of the operators available for refining your search.

Summary

When it comes to search keep these things in mind:

- Search is an art rather than an exact science
- Track your searches to avoid confusion and duplication of effort
- When you can't find what you're looking for, set up Google Alerts for the most promising searches (See Chapter 7)
- Only a fraction of the available genealogy information is currently on the Web

Remember: it's just as valuable to know what is NOT available on the Web (today, that is!) as what IS available on the Web.

CHAPTER 4
Site Search & Resurrecting Web Sites

Google Site Search

How often have you found a web site that looks like a prime candidate for having information about your family tree, only to discover that there is no search box available to search the site?

Without a search box, a page-by-page search would be required to locate pertinent genealogical information. With web sites containing hundreds if not thousands of pages, it's almost an impossible task. Thankfully, Google offers an alternative to laboriously combing through sites like these.

Site Search Syntax

Google allows you to require that your search results only come from the website that you specify. By using Google's language for special search instructions – called "syntaxes" – you can incorporate advanced search techniques right from the search box.

For example, the query ["1930 census" site:census.gov] will return pages about the 1930 census but only from the U.S. Census Bureau website at www.census.gov.

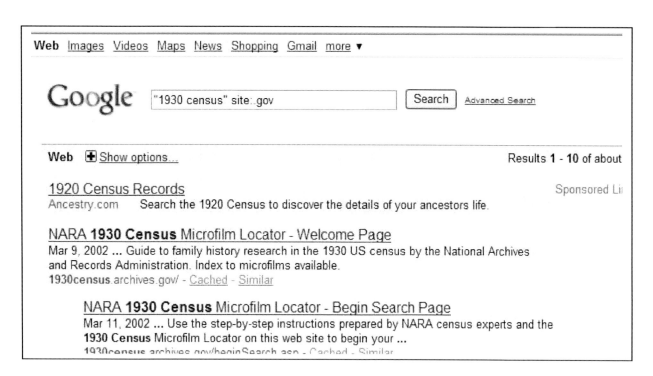

You can also specify a whole class of sites with Site search. For example, **"1930 census" site:.gov** will return results only from websites with a .gov domain (above) and **census site:.gov.uk** will return results only from .gov websites in the United Kingdom.

As with all Google searches, you can and should employ all of the search strategies and search operators to focus your search of the web site.

Sample Search

One of the best ways to understand the power of the site search and how it works is by test-driving it.

You are probably familiar with the U.S. GenWeb Project at http://www.usgenweb.org. It's a very popular free genealogy website run by volunteers all over the country. Information is arranged by state and then by county. Because each county website is created and maintained by volunteers, no two counties are set up exactly the same. It is not uncommon to find a county website with many pages and indexes that does not have a search box.

Genealogical Example:
I research my Larson family line in the town of Winthrop, in Sibley County, Minnesota. I am interested in all Larsons from that town and the surrounding area within the county. Although the Sibley County website on www.usgenweb.org has many pages and information, it does not have a search box. This means that I would have to go page by page looking for Larsons. However, Google provides a quick and easy way for me to search the site.

How to Search a Specific Website:

1. Go to http://www.usgenweb.org
2. Click on *Minnesota*
3. Click *Choose a Minnesota County* to visit link in the upper left corner
4. Click on *Links to Counties*
5. Click on *Sibley* – you will be taken to the Sibley county GenWeb Project website. As you can see there are a lot of links and databases listed, but no search box.
6. Click on the URL address for the home page of the site to highlight it
7. Copy the address by pressing Ctrl C on your keyboard or right clicking and selecting Copy
8. Go to Google.com

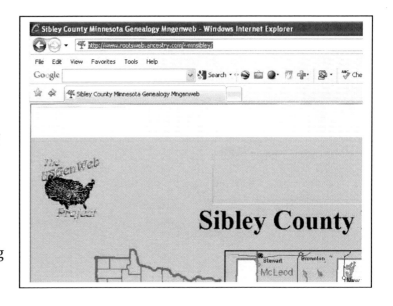

9. In the search box type LARSON SITE:
10. Immediately after the colon, paste the URL address you copied by pressing Ctrl V or by right clicking and selecting Paste
11. Click the Google Search button to conduct your search
12. The results page includes pages that include LARSON only from the Sibley County GenWeb site

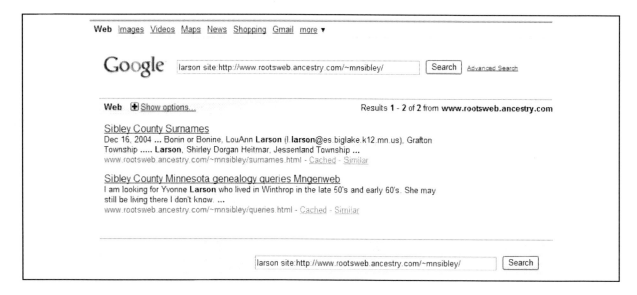

Think of the possibilities! Surnames, town names, names of businesses where your ancestors worked - the results are focused in on *your* research needs! As with all searches, you can employ all of the search strategies and operators. For example, if I had received a large number of results, I might want to revise my search as follows:

Larson + Winthrop site: http://www.rootsweb.ancestry.com/~mnsibley/

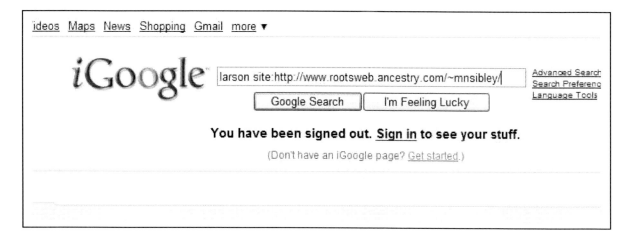

Think of the amount of time that you can save in searching websites!

Notice that the web site URL address for the Sibley county, Minnesota US GenWeb Project site has the domain name www.rootsweb.ancestry.com. This is important to note. We started on the US GenWeb Project site, but when we clicked through to the state of

Minnesota we actually left the www.usgenweb.org site and were sent to the www.rootsweb.ancestry.com web site.

This means that when we conduct a site search using the address for the Sibley County, MN site, we are only asking Google to search for our keywords in that site. It will not be searching any of the www.usgenweb.org pages. In the case of this search, that is acceptable. But if you are not getting the results you expect from a site search, take a moment to make note of where you started and which domain you are actually searching. Many website will send you to companion web sites for different content. Site search can only search one web site domain (and all of the pages that site contains) at a time.

Additional Syntax Instructions

Here's a list of additional syntax instructions that you can use to advance your searches:

Syntax instruction	Function	Example
Inurl:	Finds pages with a search word in the web address	Larson inurl:genealogy
Intitle:	Finds pages with a search word in the web page title that appears in your browser	Intitle:"Larson Genealogy"
Filetype:	Limits your search to PDF, doc, ppt (PowerPoint) or other file formats	genealogy filetype:ppt will give you PowerPoint presentations with "genealogy" in the file name
Define:	Finds the definition of the word that follows (handy for unfamiliar words and occupations that pop up in records)	Define:cooper

Putting It All Together

By combining the techniques we've covered thus far, you can create a very strong and efficient research strategy. By using this strategy you will find you have more time to spend on results rather than spending large amounts of time searching and re-searching.

Resurrecting Web Sites

Have you experienced the following scenario?

You construct a great search, which brings up a number of promising results. One of the results really catches your eye – it looks exactly like the kind of information you were searching for!

The catch?

When you click the link to access the page you get the following message…

"File Not Found"

...and your hopes are dashed.

Here's a little known fact: "File Not Found" doesn't necessarily mean the information is gone forever. You may be able to find it in the *Cache* version of the web page.

Behind the Scenes

As you know, Google "crawls" the web constantly indexing web sites. It also takes a snapshot of each page it examines and caches, or stores, the image as a back up. It's the behind-the-scenes information that Google uses to judge if a page is a good match for your search queries.

In the case of a website that no longer exists, the cache copy can use a snapshot of the website when it was still active. Practically every search result includes a *Cached* link.

When you land on a "File Note Found" error page, just click the Back button on your browser and look for a link to a "cached" copy at the end of the URL address at the end of the Google search result.

Clicking on that link will take you to the Google cached version of that web page, instead of the current version of the page. This is useful if the original page is unavailable because of:

- Internet congestion
- A down, overloaded, or just slow website (since Google's servers are typically faster than many web servers, you can often access a page's cached version faster than the page itself)
- The owner's recent removal of the page from the Web

Sometimes you can even access the cached version from a site that otherwise requires registration or a subscription.

If Google returns a link to a page that appears to have little to do with your query, or if you can't find the information you're seeking on the current version of the page, take a look at the cached version by clicking the cached link. You will then see the web page as it looked when Google last indexed it.

You'll notice that a gray header will appear at the top of the page. This provides you will the following information about the cached page you are viewing:

- The original web address of the page
- The date and time that the page you are viewing was cached
- A link to the current version of that page
- Your search terms highlighted (each word is color coded and will be highlighted throughout the page)

If you don't see a cached link in a search result, it may have been omitted because the owners of the site have requested that Google remove the cached version or not cache their content. Also, any sites Google hasn't yet indexed won't have a cache version.

Be aware that if the original page contains more than 101 kilobytes of text, the cached version of the page will consist only of the first 101 kbytes (120 kbytes for pdf files).

Summary

Before you give up on that web site that appears to be long gone, _click the cache_ and you may just get lucky!

Interested in learning more of the technical behind the scenes of caching? **VIDEO: _HTTP Caching_**
http://www.youtube.com/watch?v=MtJXwsxK7u8

CHAPTER 5
Image Search Pictures From the Past

Every day that goes by more and more images are being added to the Web. What does that mean for the genealogist? It mean your chance of finding a photo of one of your ancestors, or of the events and locations associated with their lives gets better every day. Thankfully, as the number of images on the Internet increases, so does the search technology that helps you to locate them.

Image Search

Since Google first introduced *Image Search* in December of 2001, users have been able to search for photos and images by the keywords in the filename of the image, the link text pointing to the image, and text adjacent to the image.

To illustrate the current breadth of Google Images, there are over 300 million digital photos taken every single day! Google appears to have set its sights on being the search index that has over 1 trillion images to search from. It's inevitable that there will be a wealth of genealogical and historical images tucked into those 1 trillion images, and that's what we will be searching for in this chapter.

Conducting An Image Search

Whether you're starting from the classic version of Google or your own iGoogle homepage, you can do a search of images on the Internet.

How to search for an image with Google:

1. In the very upper left corner of your screen you'll see the word "Web." Click the *Images* link next to it.
2. You will then be taken to Google's Image Search, which looks much like the classic version of Google
3. Type keywords for the image you are looking for in the Search box
4. Click the Search Images button

Search Results will include:
- thumbnail size images
- the name of the image
- the image size
- a link to the page on the Web that contains the image

To find photos of specific people, try putting their first and last names within quotes (i.e. "George Washington"). If you are researching an ancestor's surname that is less common (i.e. Sporowski) then you could just enter the name and that should get you started.

It's important to remember that Image Search is not limited to photographs of people. Here are some ideas for photographs worth searching that could enhance your family history research:
- Places where your ancestors lived and visited (buildings, roads, landmarks)
- Recorded events (i.e.: The Great San Francisco Earthquake of 1906)
- Cemeteries and tombstones
- Photos of heirlooms

Images are also not limited to photographs. You can use the Google image search to find:
- Maps
- Drawings
- Paintings
- Old postcards
- Charts and graphs
- Clipart

Below: The results of an image search on the keyword genealogy. Note the variety of images.

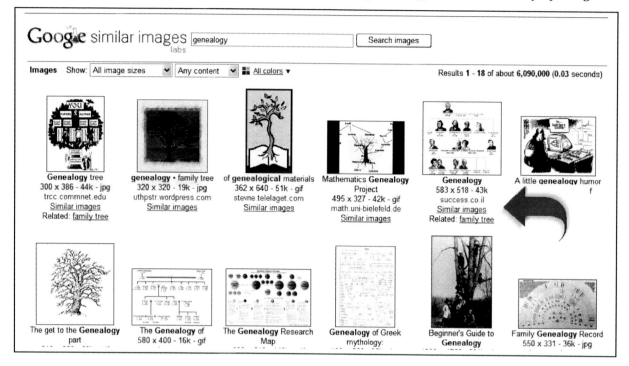

Search Example

Let's say the Work Projects Administration employed one of your ancestors during the Great Depression and you want to search for images of WPA workers. Type "WPA worker" in the search box and click the Search Images button. Your results list will include many historic images related to the WPA.

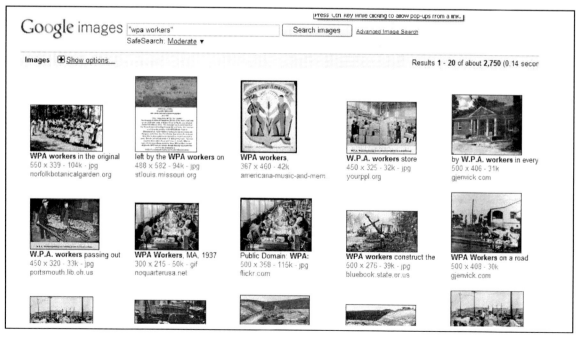

As with any Google search, all of the search operators and syntax can be incorporated to focus your image search.

Advanced Search

It's inevitable that when you do an image search, you will end up with some images that don't appear to have anything to do with what you were searching for. To address this problem, Google is incorporating some of the best *Object Recognition Technology* available.

> ***Object Recognition Technology*** *(from Wikipedia): Object recognition in computer vision (computer vision is the science and technology of machines that see) is the task of finding a given object in an image or video sequence.*

This technology can help you narrow down the results to meet your specifications. You can tap into this tool with Google's Advanced Search. Let's look at an example of how this works.

Go to Image Search and look for a portrait of a historical figure such as George Washington. Type in "George Washington" and click the Search Images button.

In the results pages you will see many faces of George Washington.

However, as you move on through the search results, soon you'll come across a photograph of George Washington's false teeth. Not exactly what you were looking for.

(Image Below: On the left are George Washington's False Teeth)

George Washington's
500 x 375 - 115k - jpg
flickr.com

George Washington wore
420 x 607 - 64k
coloradosprings.yourhub.com

To eliminate the unwanted images and narrow in on the desired images, go back to the search box and click the Advanced Image Search link.

Image Below: the arrow points to the Advanced Image Search link

You'll see a blue box near the top and then a white box below. Within that white box the first option is *Content Types: return images that contain*. This is where object recognition technology now can come in to play.

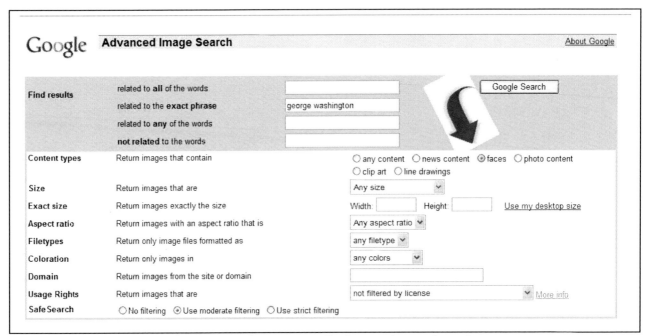

Image Above: note the variety of advanced search options.

Click the *Faces* button and then click the Google Search button again.

Now every search result is a facial image. It may be a portrait on a stamp or on a coin, but it will be a face. We have succeeded in narrowing the original search results down from 6,720,000 to 548,000 images of faces. Think how well this might work with an ancestor who is not quite is famous as George Washington!

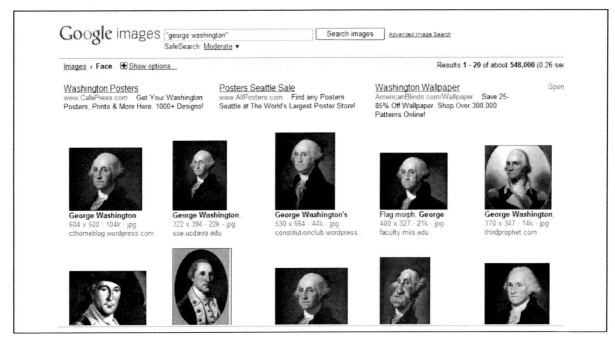

It is still possible that some of the results may not be George Washington's face. For example, the results may include an image of the face of someone who works at George Washington University because this technology has not yet been perfected. However, Google has made a commitment to start adding features that use complex image analysis. In the future, this may mean that once you've homed in on the face you're looking for, Google will be able to detect it specifically and narrow your results even further. This technology already exists and is currently being used by law enforcement agencies.

This evolving technology offers powerful possibilities for genealogists in the future. Think of the Dead Fred website at http://www.deadfred.com. There are thousands of faces in vintage photographs on the Dead Fred web site that are currently unidentified. But what if some day we could do a facial recognition search on a known ancestor and be able to pull in results of unidentified faces from other web sites that match? Faces that were once unknown may turn out to be yet another portrait of one of your ancestors!

Photo *tags* could also potentially assist with identification of vintage photographs.

When we look at a vintage photo, we are often able to determine where the people in the photo were from based on the photographer's name and location on the back of the image or on the edges of a cabinet card.

In today's world, this same type of information – location, names, dates – can be *tagged* onto digital photos.

In the case of images of unknown ancestor photos, we could potentially search utilizing face recognition technology in conjunction with photo information tags.

Google doesn't plan on limiting image recognition to just the faces of people. In the future, you will be seeing an ability to find objects in photographs and use them as a reliable benchmark for filtering irrelevant images. This might come in handy if you are looking for a particular landmark or item that pertains to your research.

Another feature we can expect to see more of in the future from Google is *GPS Enabled Encoding*. With 300 million digital images being snapped every day, it may prove very helpful to actually encode the photo with the exact geographic location where that camera phone or digital camera was located when it snapped the photo.

What could this mean for your genealogy research? In the case of an image search for an ancestor's tombstone it could make quite a difference. The author of a web page may have neglected to give complete source information as to where the photograph was taken or not labeled the photo in such a way that a regular Google image search would bring it up in search results. But Google may still be able to locate the image for you based on the geographic location encoded into the digital image.

And finally, Google has developed an improved algorithm for ranking images in order of their relevance to your specific search called VisualRank.

> **VisualRank** *is a system for finding and ranking images by analyzing and comparing their content, rather than searching image names, Web links, or other text.*

We should continue to see ongoing improvements on image results. However, all of this innovation costs money. So expect to see the addition of image display ads next to image results. The good news is that you'll be more likely to come across image ads when doing queries for commercial items, rather than historic photos. Google has promised to keep ads low key and not detracting from the user experience.

Pictures From The Past

Has this happened to you? You conduct an image search and locate a great image that would be ideal for your research only to click on the image and get the following page:

If you click on the thumbnail image in your search results and the image is no longer available, there may be another way to retrieve it.

As we discussed in Chapter 4, Google is constantly "crawling" the web and indexing web pages and images to include in the results of your searches. Each time a web page or image is crawled, Google caches the page.

Because Google doesn't crawl for images as often as it does for Web pages, you may find an image has moved or been removed since the last time Google indexed the web site where it resided. This means you may be able to locate the missing image from the older cached version of the web site.

How to Retrieve an Image That is No Longer Available:

1. Use your mouse to highlight the URL website address that appears below the thumbnail image in the search results
2. Press CTRL C on your keyboard to copy the address
3. Click the "Web" link above the Google search box to go back to website searches
4. Place your curser in the search box by clicking inside it
5. Press CTRL V on your keyboard, which will paste the URL address into the search box
6. Click the Search button
7. The first few results should be from the web site that had the image you wanted
8. Look at the last line of the result for that web site and click on the *cache* link

9. Now you are looking at a cache version of the web site where the image once appeared. Browse through the site and look for the image. If you're lucky the version of the web site that you are viewing was saved <u>before</u> the image was removed, and the image may still be there.

Image Below: Paste the URL address of the cached web site in the Web search box.

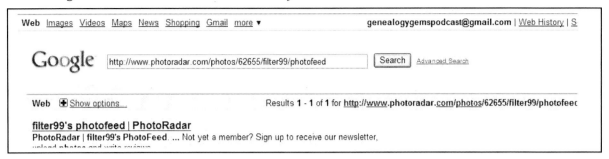

This may sound like a lot of effort, but when only that missing image will do, you will be glad to have this little search technique in your skill toolbox.

Similar Images

Google is constantly developing new search techniques, but in the early stages of their development you won't find them integrated into the standard Google Image search. Instead, you will most likely find the early "beta versions" at the Google Labs website at http://www.googlelabs.com/.

The designers at Google are currently cooking up some new advances in Image Search. One that you will definitely want to try is the *Similar Images* search.

According to the Google Labs web site, "Similar Images allows you to search for images using pictures rather than words. Click the "Similar images" link under an image to find other images that look like it."

The best way to see the value in the Similar Images Search is to give it a test run.

How To Do A Similar Images Search:

1. Go to http://similar-images.googlelabs.com/
2. Do an Image search on the word *genealogy*
3. The results will include many familiar images like trees, charts, vintage photos, cartoons, collages, ancient artwork, and more.

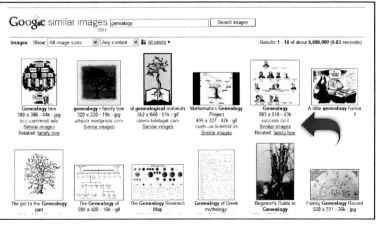

4. Select the image you think most closely matches what you are looking for and click the "Similar Images" link beneath the image.

5. Instantly your results will change from a wide variety of images to results that closely resemble the image you selected. Now all of the results are similar to the one you selected.

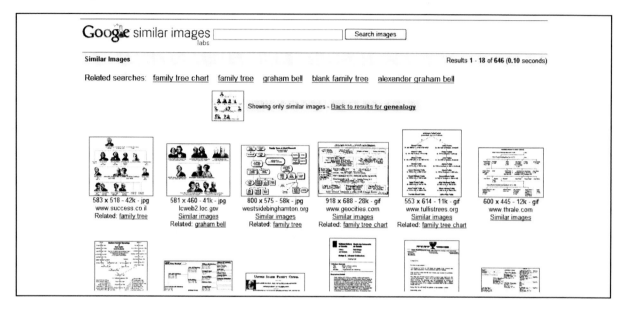

Let's look at another genealogy themed example.

Suppose that you've just discovered that your great great grandfather was a blacksmith and you'd like to find a vintage image of a blacksmith for a report. You could go from web site to web site hoping that you'll come across what you are looking for – OR – you could do a Google Labs Similar Image Search.

Conduct a Similar Images search on *Blacksmith.*

You'll notice that not every image has a "Similar Images" link beneath the image. The image came up because of how it was labeled (i.e. "Blacksmith") but Google's Similar Search may not be sure how to categorize that particular image. But in most cases you will find a Similar Images link.

Click on the Similar Images link for the one that best meets your needs. In this case, we will select a vintage photograph of a Blacksmith inside his shop.

Now you have a number of results that all are similar in appearance and theme to the image you selected. Once you find the photograph you want, you can click through to the web site to determine the copyright restrictions or contact the webmaster for more information about the image.

Similar Images could be a very fast and effective tool for reviewing image options from across the Internet.

More Image Search Tips

- If you come across a name in your genealogy research and are unsure if the first name is a man's name or a woman's name, conduct a search on that name and the images will likely answer the question.

- If you don't know the meaning of a word do an image search and the pictures may assist you.

- To quickly assess the contents of a web site search the images: On the Advanced Image Search page enter the address of the web site that you want to search in the *Domain - Return images from the site or domain* search box.

- When conducting Similar Images searches, experiment with the Search Options Column. You can sort results by:
  - Image Size
  - Type
  - Color

To see a quick review of Google Similar Images watch…
VIDEO: *Similar Images Demo*
http://www.youtube.com/watch?v=6fD2t4d2Ln4

Looking to the Future

If you are interested in reading more about what the future may hold for Image Search at Google, read the blog post *Future Update for Google Image Search* at the *Google Operating System Blog:* http://googlesystem.blogspot.com/2008/05/future-updates-for-google-image-search.html

CHAPTER 6
Google Alerts

Since information is being uploaded to the Web constantly, it's nearly impossible to keep up on new web pages that may contain information about your family tree. By setting up a Google Alert for the searches you have already conducted, you won't have to go out every day on the Web and search for that topic to see if there is anything new. Instead, Google will do the work for you. Google Alerts is like having your own research assistant!

Google Alerts are emails automatically sent to you when there are new Google results for your search terms. You can also have your alerts delivered to you via a feed to the feed reader of your choice (e.g., Google Reader or add the feed to your iGoogle page).

Creating Google Alerts

Let's look at an example search:

Larson AND Winthrop AND Minnesota

How To Set Up a Google Alert for a Search:

Go to: http://www.google.com/alerts
(Remember: you must be signed in to your Google account to set up alerts.)

In the *Create a Google Alert* box we'll type in the search terms:
Ex: Larson AND Winthrop AND Minnesota

You will find that you can select the type of search that you want Google to conduct. In most cases you will want to conduct a Comprehensive search, which will cause Google to search all types of websites. However, there might be other occasions where you would want to select one of the other categories:

- News
- Blogs
- Web
- Video
- Groups

For example, you may want to follow a story about the possible closing of a library in your area in the news. In that case you would select News as the type of results that you want.

You can also select how often you want to receive search results. If you have several Google alerts or if it's a topic where there is a lot of new information being published, you may want to select Once A Day or even Once A Week. But you can also select As-It-Happens to receive results the moment they are found.

Your final option is to choose where you would like your Google Alert delivered. You can choose to have them sent to the email address for your Google account, or you can have them sent to a Feed (which will be discussed later in this chapter).

When you're done, click the Create Alert button. You will automatically be taken to your Manage Your Alerts console.

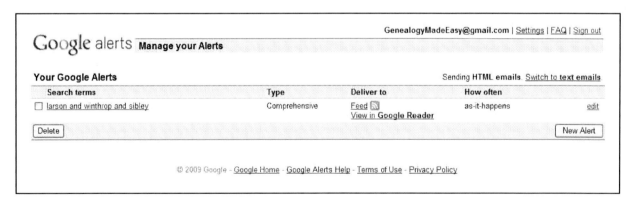

This is where you will find and edit all of the alerts you have created. The alerts are listed alphabetically. Currently, you can have up to 1000 alerts.

If you chose to have your alert delivered to a feed rather than an email, you will see a link that says FEED in the *Deliver To* column along with a small orange RSS button. Directly beneath it is a link that allows you to go to Google Reader to see your feed.

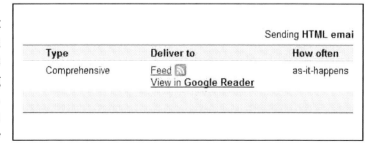

www.GenealogyGems.com

Click the link and you will see your alert listed, probably with no new results listed yet since the alert is brand new. But each day as Google locates new results, they will show up in the Google Reader where you can click through to the page that was found.

Google Reader is not the only "feed aggregator" that you can use to receive your alerts. By copying and pasting the RSS for your alert into your favorite feed aggregator you can follow them where you want.

How to Add a Google Alert Feed to Another Feed Aggregator:

1. Go to http://www.google.com/alerts
2. Click the *Click here to manage your alerts* link
3. Click the Feed link or the orange RSS button for the alert you want to add
4. Click on the URL address for that feed page to highlight the address
5. Copy the address to your computer's clipboard
6. Go to the Feed Aggregator of your choice
7. Paste the feed address

Let's look at an example of how to add an alert feed to an iGoogle feed aggregator gadget:

How to Add a Google Alert Gadget to Your iGoogle Home Page:

1. Follow the instructions above, highlighting the feed address
2. Go to your iGoogle page (if you have created an iGoogle page you just need to be signed into your Google account and go to http://www.google.com)
3. Click the *Add Stuff* link in the upper right corner of the page
4. At the bottom of the left column click the *Add Feed or Gadget* link
5. Paste the feed address into the pop up box
6. Click the *Add* button
7. A yellow bar will appear indicating that a feed gadget has been added to your iGoogle page
8. Click the *back to iGoogle home* link at the upper right corner of the page
9. You will now find a new Google Alert gadget in the upper left corner of your gadget area with the title of

the Google alert search. As new results for that Google alert are found they will appear as links in your gadget.

Editing Google Alerts

Over time you may decide that you want to receive emails rather than follow the alert on a feed. Or you may find that you are not receiving as many alerts as you expected and you want to change the search terms. All editing of alerts is done in the Alerts Management Console.

How to Edit a Google Alert:

1. Go to http://www.google.com/alerts
2. Click the *Click here to manage your alerts* link
3. Locate the alert you want to edit in the alphabetical list and click the *Edit* link on the far right side of the alert
4. The line for that alert will be highlighted in yellow and all of the elements of the alert will available for editing. Note: if your alert is set to go to a feed, *How Often* will not be an option. Frequency is only applicable to receiving alerts by email.
5. When you're done making changes click the *Save* button for that alert

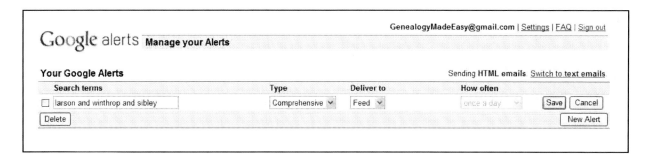

If you do receive your alerts by email, they will appear in HTML format. If you want to receive a simpler text version of the emails, click the *Switch to Text Emails* link in the upper right corner of your Manage Your Alerts console.

Alerts That Will Further Your Research

Now that you know how to create and manage your alerts, let's discuss what types of alerts might benefit your genealogy research.

Certainly, any search that you might conduct for your research is a candidate for a Google alert. But there are additional sources for alerts to consider as part of your research strategy.

Do you have an ancestor's journal? Consider transcribing it or making a photocopy of it. With your highlighter pen go through and highlight names, places, business names, occupations, addresses, schools attended, churches attended, etc. These are all keywords worthy of searches and Google Alerts.

How about setting up a Google Alert for each surname you are researching in a particular area? Here are a few examples from my own Google Alerts and research:

Cooke + Huntingdonshire
Cooke + Brampton + England
Sporan + Chowchilla
Larson + Winthrop + Sibley County

Again, you will need to focus your search a bit more for common surnames. Keep it simpler for more rare surnames that won't generate as many results. Refer back to the search strategies from the previous chapters.

How about the neighbors? Pull out the census or the City Directory for your ancestors and set up a few targeted Google alerts that might give you more information about your ancestor's community and the people they were closest to.

The options are only limited by the 1000 alert limit that Google applies.

For a visual overview of setting up Google Alerts watch...
VIDEO: *Google Alerts by the Arlington Heights Memorial Library*
http://www.youtube.com/watch?v=Tzby81W92w4

CHAPTER 7
Gmail

Not Just Another Email Service

Though millions of people use Gmail, only a small fraction are using it to its full capacity. For the genealogist, those unused capabilities can make the difference between being efficient and getting lost in a mountain of email.

If you already have a free Google account, you can use that same account to create a Gmail account. Even though you may already have another email provider, go ahead and set up a Gmail account. The account is free and doesn't require anything more than a user name and password.

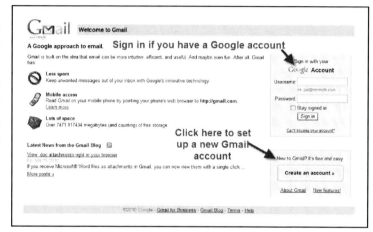

To set up a free Gmail account simply do a Google search for Gmail and click the link in the results page or go to www.google.com/mail

Archiving

Chances are you get a lot of email and if it's related to your family history research, you probably want to save it for later reference. In many email systems emails are saved to folders, which have some inherent problems:

- You can only save the email to one topic folder
- The folder may become so full that you lose track of individual emails
- The subject of the folder may evolve over time and in order to break out a segment of emails on a secondary subject you would have to go through each email and save it to a new folder

And the list goes on...

With Gmail, folders are a thing of the past. Gmail emails are archived using a tagging system, similar to how you might tag a multitude of subjects for a blog post or photograph. Once tagged, you can retrieve your email in the future by clicking the label in the left hand column. When there are a large number of emails, thin the results by using the Gmail search engine and searching additional keywords. Let's look at an example of an email you might receive:

There is only one family story that I ever heard growing up. That was the immigration story of my Great-Grandpa Norman Jacobson, from Steigen, Norway. When Norman's father (a fisherman) died of pneumonia around 1905, Norman's mother could not find enough work to support a family, so they immigrated in 1906. His mother, Charlotte, or "Lottie" as she was referred to, brought her 5 children to Minnesota and settled in Cottonwood County.

When I first heard of the Ellis Island site, I excitedly searched the database only to get messages like, "too many to list." Several months later I was searching USGenWeb's site looking for Minnesota indexes where I came across the Iron Mountain Range Genealogy Website. A search on their index brought up both Charlotte and Norman. They both appeared in the 1918 Alien Registration Index of Minnesota, and had also filed Naturalization papers in Minnesota. Of course, I was ecstatic. When the records arrived, they confirmed the family did arrive in 1906. Armed with this new proof, I headed back to Ellis Island.

This email refers to several topics of interest:
- A family surname
- A county where you do a significant amount of research
- Ellis Island

Rather than having to try to decide on just one folder, Gmail allows you to tag the email with as many labels as you want.

How To Add A Label To An Email

1. Open the email in Gmail
2. Click the LABELS button above the email
3. Select a label you have already created from the drop down list or select CREATE NEW
4. If creating a new label, a NEW LABEL box will pop up. Type the label name and click OK

www.GenealogyGems.com

As you add labels, they appear alphabetically in the column on the left. If you have several they may not all show up. Instead you will see the ones you use most often and then a link to the number of additional labels you have and the word "more." Just click that link and all the labels become visible.

Once you have labeled the email simply click the ARCHIVE button at the top of the email and Gmail will tuck it away out of sight.

To retrieve the email, click one of the labels on the left that you tagged it with and it will appear in a results list containing all of the emails with that label.

Notice the words now appearing in the Gmail search box:

"label: ellis-island"

Gmail is indicating that the emails listed are tagged "ellis-island."

As you work with Gmail chances are you will want to add, edit, and remove labels. There are several ways to do this.

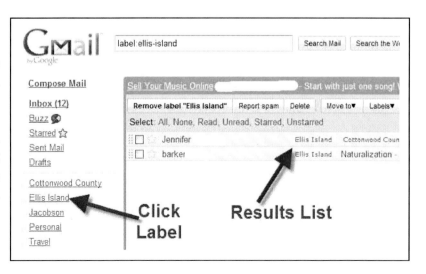

Option 1) Select MANAGE LABELS in the left column.
(If MANAGE LABELS doesn't appear, click the MORE link, which will reveal all of your labels, as well as the MANAGE LABELS link.)

Option 2) Click the SETTINGS link in the upper right corner and clicking the LABELS tab.

It is here in the Labels tab under Settings where you can select which labels are:
- Shown in the left column
- Hidden so they don't appear in the left column
- Removed

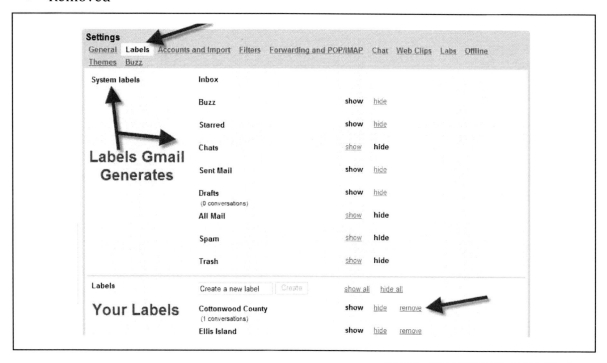

Option 3) Edit labels directly in the left column. Click the light colored box just to the left of the label name you want to edit. In addition to hiding and deleting the label, you can:

- Rename the label
- Add a custom color to the label

Color-coding your labels can help you stay organized as your list of labels grows. Consider coloring prominent surnames you are researching, or simply using one color for all genealogy-related labels. Customize as you go to suit your needs and make it easier to spot the label you want.

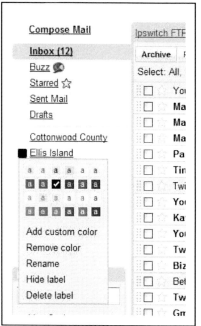

www.GenealogyGems.com

The Power of Search

The really unique feature of Gmail is the dedicated search box. As frequent Google users it can be very easy to overlook the search box and not realize that it is not just a "Google search" box, but also a "Gmail search" box.

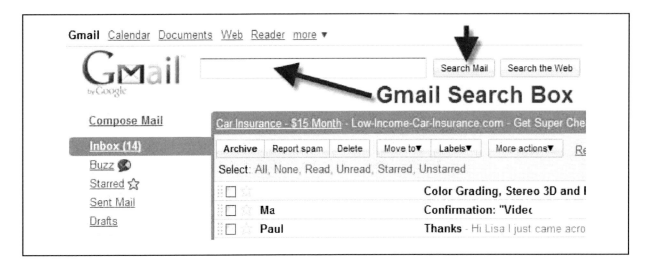

Why is this Gmail search box so important? The answer is simple: you may never lose track of another email message again…ever!

Let's say that you just found a key research document and you realize that it ties in with a genealogical theory that a distant cousin wrote you about months ago. You want to retrieve the email and review it with the new information. But you have had hundreds of emails from that cousin and can't remember when you received it. No problem! Simply type in the Gmail search box a keyword or two about the topic of the email, click SEARCH MAIL, and Gmail will retrieve it for you.

In the example above, the topic of the email was "naturalization" and Gmail instantly pulled up two emails from a year ago that contain that keyword.

You can also incorporate all of the search techniques and operators used in regular searches including:

- Quotations marks to specify an exact phrase
- Plus sign to indicate a word that must be included
- Minus sign to eliminate unwanted words
- The tilde symbol to search for a word or it's synonyms (i.e. ~train also retrieves railroad and locomotive)
- Asterisk between two keywords indicating the words may be separated by one or more words. (i.e. President * Lincoln)

The Gmail search box is the fastest way to retrieve an archived email. However, if you wish to browse emails that have a particular label, click on the label in the column on the left and all archived emails with that label will appear. And once again, the label also appears in the search box. Google does this in case you would like to search within that set of labeled results. This comes in very handy when you have a large number or emails tagged with a certain label.

To search within labeled results, type additional keywords (and operators if needed) following the label text in the box and click the SEARCH MAIL button.

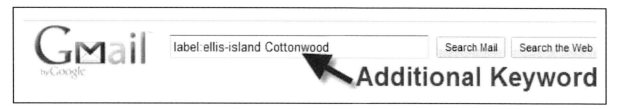

This search method makes it possible to pull up potentially hundreds of archived emails with a label and with lightening speed narrow it down to just a specific few!

At any time while in your Gmail account, Google search is just a click away. Type your search query into the box and click the SEARCH THE WEB button.

Conversation Threads

When it comes to genealogy, understanding the context of information is critical. And when it comes to genealogy-related emails, it is not uncommon to have multiple emails back and forth on a subject. Gmail makes these online conversations very easy to follow with conversation threads. These are much like the threads you find on genealogy

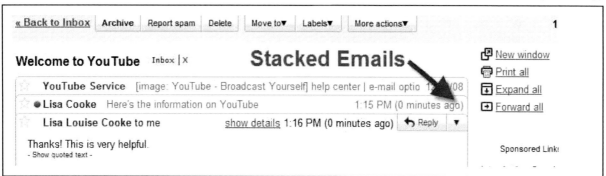

message boards like Rootsweb.

Rather than wading through all your email trying to follow a conversation, Gmail replies to replies (and so on). They are all displayed in the order received, all in one place, making it easier to understand the context of the messages, and creating a true conversation.

When you open an email message in a conversation, all of your related messages will be stacked on top of each other in order. This is called Conversation View. To see all the messages included in the conversation click the EXPAND ALL link.

To collapse the thread click COLLAPSE ALL.

Be aware that if you change the subject line, or if the conversation exceeds 100 messages, the conversation will break off into a new thread.

See it in Action!
VIDEO: *5 Ways Gmail Makes Life Easier: Conversation Chains*
http://www.youtube.com/user/google?blend=2&ob=4#p/search/14/xu_sKuhg05o

Working Offline

One of the more recent features of Gmail is the ability to work offline. It is inevitable that at some point the Internet will temporarily go down or you will find your self on a plane or other location where an Internet connection is unavailable. With the offline feature those down times become an opportunity to catch up on your backlog of email.

Activate offline Gmail from the OFFLINE tab under Settings and Gmail will download a local cache of your mail, which synchronizes with Gmail's servers while you're connected. When you lose connectivity, Gmail automatically switches to offline mode so you can keep working. You can even continue to compose email replies because they will be automatically sent the next time Gmail detects a connection.

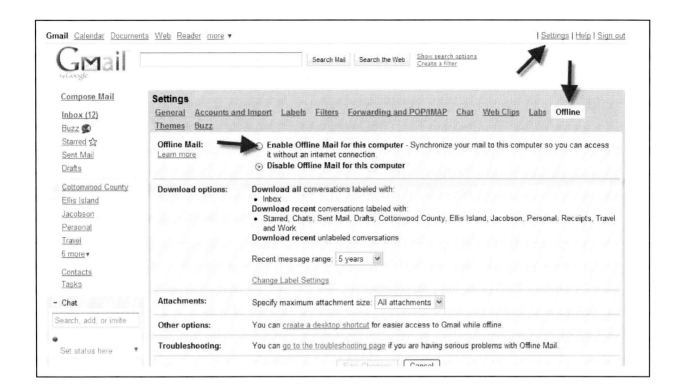

Spam Filter

No matter how good an email client system is, there will always be spam - that unwanted email often from shady characters. The good news is that Gmail has an excellent spam system built around the same premise as their search engine, which means it's good at discerning content. Gmail has a great track record for accurately labeling and archiving spam email so that you never have to be bothered with it in your inbox. For the occasional messages that do slip through Gmail's filter, it's easy to report the spam and get rid of it. The more spam you mark, the better Google will get at weeding out those annoying messages.

How To Remove Spam From Your Inbox:

1. Click the checkbox next to each unwanted SPAM email message
2. Click the REPORT SPAM button at the top of the email box

How To Remove Spam Forever:

1. **Option 1**: On the left side of the Gmail page click the SPAM label. (If you don't see the SPAM label, click MORE above the CONTACTS label on the left side of the page)
2. Select the messages you'd like to

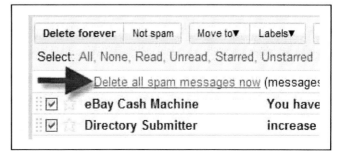

delete and click DELETE FOREVER

3. **Option 2**: Delete <u>everything</u> by clicking DELETE ALL SPAM MESSAGES NOW
4. If you or Google accidentally marks a legitimate message as spam, click NOT SPAM at the top of the message. If you just marked it as spam, you can also click UNDO immediately after to recover the message.

QUICK TIP: To help avoid having a wanted email go to the spam folder, add the sender's email address to your Contact list.

See It In Action!
VIDEO: *5 Ways Gmail Makes Life Easier: Spam Protection*
http://www.youtube.com/user/google?blend=2&ob=4#p/search/23/LhlrsJ-PaQw

Fun With Themes

Adding a theme to your Gmail may not help you get through your emails any faster, but it might just make the job a little more pleasant.

VIDEO*: 5 Ways Gmail Makes Life Easier: Themes*
http://www.youtube.com/user/google?blend=2&ob=4#p/search/19/ucDePBBlNSM

How To Add A Theme To Gmail:

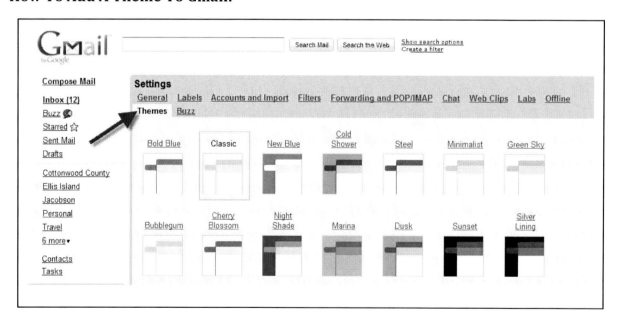

1. Click the SETTINGS link in the upper right hand corner of Gmail
2. Click on the theme of your choice or select Choose Your Own Colors
3. The new theme will be instantly applied to your Gmail account

An example of a fun new Gmail theme:

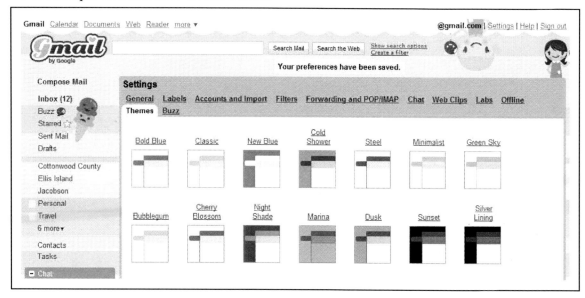

www.GenealogyGems.com

CHAPTER 8
iGoogle - Your Personal Genealogy Homepage

In this chapter you are going to jump into the driver's seat by creating your own custom Google homepage. iGoogle is the nifty way to customize the Google homepage to be your own personal genealogy search "dashboard." iGoogle puts everything at your fingertips to help you maneuver the Internet as effectively as possible. By creating a personalized genealogy homepage that facilitates your family history research, you are going to get even more out of your precious research time.

The homepage will include what are called "gadgets," little windows that each carry out a specific online task. Some gadgets will give you daily genealogy news, some will be more practical like research to-do lists, little reminder sticky notes, your Google notebook, and a listing of your top genealogy bookmarks. The beauty of iGoogle is that you are going to pick and choose each gadget so that your homepage is set up and ready to go to help keep you organized, focused, informed, and successful!

One note before we begin: Please keep in mind that iGoogle appears and behaves differently on each computer and with each browser. Google may also make changes to the interface without notice.

Creating Your iGoogle Page

Execute these steps as you go through this lesson and you will have a completed iGoogle page by the end.

How to Create Version 1.0 of Your iGoogle Page:

1. Go to http://google.com
2. Click the Sign In link
3. Sign in with your Google account username and password
4. Once you are signed in, Google will still look the same, but you will now see a link to iGoogle in the upper right corner. Click the iGoogle link.

Here is approximately what your screen will now look like:

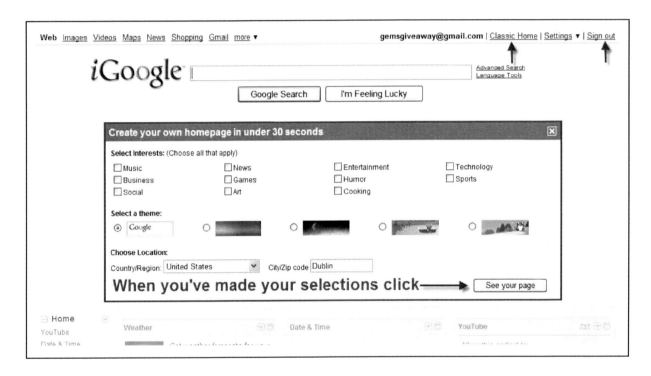

In the upper right corner you'll notice that you're just one click away from the classic version of the Google webpage. So you always have the option to use iGoogle or classic. You'll also find the Sign Out link. Click the link and you will simply be using the classic version of Google with no iGoogle link. This is handy if you share your computer with others.

Commonly Asked iGoogle Questions:

Q: Can my spouse and I have our own iGoogle homepages on the same computer?
A: Yes! Just create your own iGoogle while signed in to your personal account. Sign out when you are not using it and your spouse can sign in.

Q: Does iGoogle reside on my computer?
A: No. You are creating a customized webpage on the Google website. The benefit to this is that you don't use precious hard drive space on your computer, and you can access your iGoogle account from any computer anywhere.

On this page you also have the option to indicate personal interests that will prompt Google to automatically assign gadgets to your page. Leave those unchecked for now. You can also select one of the themes, but wait on that as well because there are thousands of themes to choose from and we will cover that later in the chapter. For now, just click the SAVE YOUR PAGE button. Here's what you'll get:

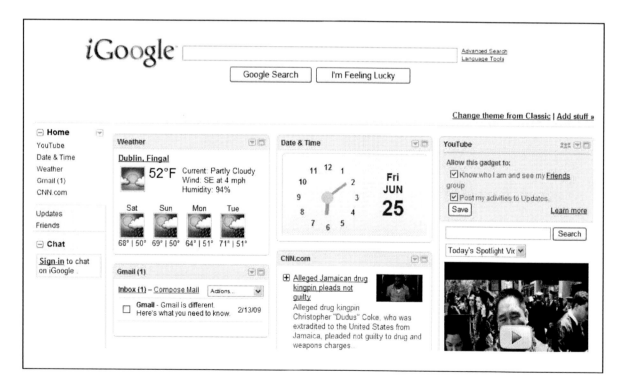

iGoogle starts you off with a handful of gadgets automatically.

How to Delete Gadgets You Don't Want

1. Click the Down Arrow button in the upper right corner of the gadget you wish to remove
2. Select Delete This Gadget from the drop down menu
3. You'll be asked if you are sure you want to delete the gadget and Click OK
4. The gadget will disappear. There will be a yellow box under the Google search box indicating which gadget you removed and offering an Undo button in case you change your mind.

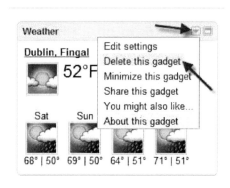

Take a moment at this point to remove gadgets that you don't want.

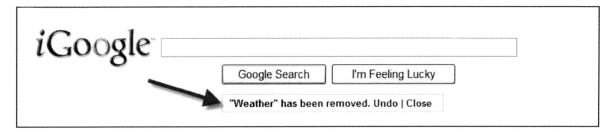

Make iGoogle Your Homepage

Before you begin customizing iGoogle, you are going to make it the Homepage for your Internet browser. This way you will always be just one click away from everything you need to do your research online. There are several different Internet browsers available, but we will cover Internet Explorer for the PC and Safari for the Mac. If you use a different browser, the steps should be fairly similar. Consult HELP on your browser and search for help on "homepage."

How to Make iGoogle Your Homepage on Internet Explorer:

1. While on your iGoogle page, click the down arrow next to the house icon on the bar across the top of the browser
2. Select ADD OR CHANGE HOME PAGE from the drop down menu
3. In the pop up window select "use this webpage as your only home page"
4. Click the YES button

How to Make iGoogle Your Homepage on Safari:

1. While on your iGoogle page, click SAFARI at the top of your browser
2. Select PREFERENCES

www.GenealogyGems.com

3. Select the GENERAL icon
4. Type http://www.google.com/ in the home page field in the pop up box
5. Close the box

Now when you click the house icon on your browser you will automatically be taken to your iGoogle homepage. As you add gadgets you will see what an advantage it will be to have one click access to your homepage and how it will help you keep your research focused and organized.

Adding Genealogy Gadgets

Now that you have a fairly clean slate, it's time to add genealogy gadgets.

How to Add Genealogy Gadgets:

1. Click the ADD STUFF link on the right side of the page.

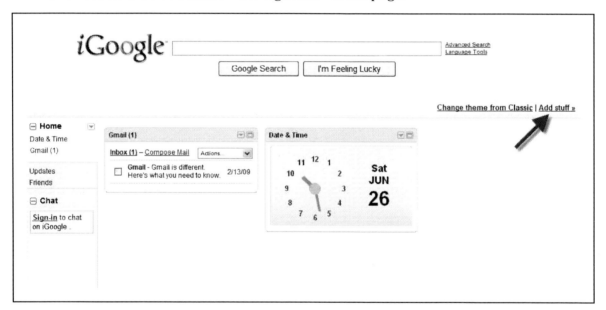

2. You are now on the "Gadgets" directory page
3. In the SEARCH FOR GADGETS box on the right type GENEALOGY
4. Click the SEARCH button
5. Now you have pages of results for genealogy themed gadgets. Find one that interests you and click the ADD IT NOW button below the gadget icon. The button will turn yellow and say ADDED.
6. Your gadget is now already on your iGoogle homepage. Click the HOME button on your browser to see the new gadget.

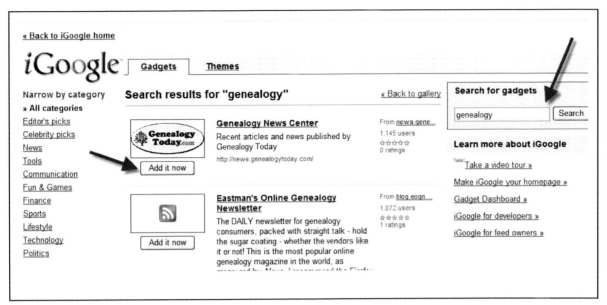

Image Above: Search for Genealogy Gadgets and click the Add It Now button.

Image Below: The Gadget has been added to your iGoogle page.

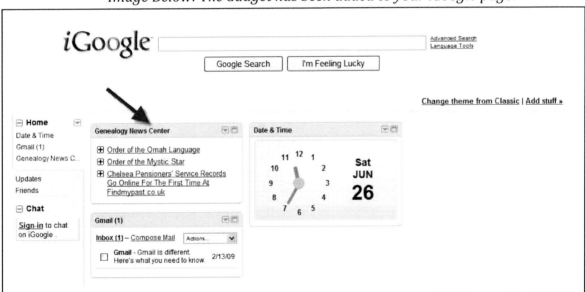

Continue to look for genealogy-themed gadgets by clicking ADD STUFF and searching the Gadget Gallery.

(Note: Gadgets are submitted to the gallery by companies as well as individuals. Occasionally gadgets are abandoned by the developer, or a new gadget will be issued on the same subject. If you add a gadget that doesn't work properly, simply delete it and continue searching through the gallery. Gadgets may also be removed without notice.)

Genealogy Related Gadgets You May Want to Try:

☐ *About.com Genealogy* – Popular "How To" Genealogy Blog

☐ *American Memory Search* – Search the documents in the Library of Congress' American Memory collections.

☐ *Bureau of Land Management Patent Search* – Searches the website

☐ *Eastman's Online Genealogy Newsletter* – Long-time source for genealogy news

☐ *FamilySearch* – (by http://hosting.gmodules.com) Searches the FamilySearch website.

☐ *GEDCOM Search* – this might be fun to play with

☐ *Genealogy Blog* – this gadget is produced by Everton Publishers and shows you links to blog articles.

☐ *Genealogy Blog Finder* – This gadget is great for finding blogs that mention a particular genealogical topic of interest.

☐ *Genealogy Help* – This gadget is linked to a website. It's not clear who runs it, but something of interest may pop up now and again.

☐ *Genealogy Insider* – Brings you the latest posts by Family Tree Magazine.

☐ *Genealogy News* – hosted by a website called topix.com.

☐ *Today in History* – A fun read. There's also a Daily US Civil War History gadget and a Daily World War II history gadget.

☐ *24-7 Family History Circle* – hosted by Ancestry.com

☐ *Worldcat Search* – Searches the world's libraries right from iGoogle.

In addition to genealogy-themed gadgets there are several gadgets specific to tools provided by Google that you wouldn't want to miss:

Google Gadgets:

☐ *Google Book Search Library* – Search and preview books, create a Library, and receive personalized book recommendations. A must for genealogists!

☐ *Google Bookmarks* – Keep links to all your favorite Genealogy websites in one gadget.

☐ *Google Calendar* – Keep track of deadlines, follow-ups and dates.

☐ *Google Docs* – View your active Google documents.

☐ *GMAIL Inbox* – GMAIL is Google's free email service. This gadget let's you see incoming mail whenever you are on your homepage. Gmail has some unique features, which makes it ideal for genealogists.

☐ *Google Map Search* – A great tool for looking up ancestor addresses.

☐ *Google Notebook* – ideal for family research.

☐ *Google Reader* – View your Google Reader items and read any RSS or Atom feed.

☐ *YouTube Search* - Episode #4 of the *Genealogy Gems Podcast* will teach you all about YouTube and how to find family history related videos. This is a great way to have them at your fingertips.

☐ *Google Tip of the Day* – Learn new ways to use Google every day.

☐ *Google Tools* – Create a custom list of the Google tools you use most giving you one-click access.

☐ *Google Translate* – Translates between common languages.

Other "Desktop" Gadgets That Might Prove Useful:

☐ *Alarm Clock* – There are several to choose from. Digital and Analogue styles.

☐ *My To Do List* – Prioritizes to-do items as Low, Med & High. Easy to edit and delete when accomplished.

☐ *Mapquest* – Several to choose from providing directions and maps.

☐ *Sticky Note* – (by Google.com) Edit the title to customize. Add several for different areas of your research.

☐ *Tiny URL Creator* – Need to send someone the URL address to a great genealogy website but it's really long? Copy and paste it into this gadget to get a nice short address to send.

```
Sticky Note                    ▼ ☐

Surname:  LARSON
County: Sibley
Census years checked:
|1790 - 1840
Next to check: 1850
```

Genealogy Podcast and Blog Gadgets

Your iGoogle homepage wouldn't really be devoted to genealogy if it didn't include gadgets for your favorite genealogy blogs and podcasts. Since most of these websites don't have their own iGoogle gadget, you will need to set them up yourself.

How to Add Genealogy Blog and Podcast Gadgets:

1. Start on your iGoogle home page
2. Go to the genealogy blog or podcast website that you want to add. For this example, go to my *Genealogy Gems News* Blog at http://genealogygemspodcast.blogspot.com/
3. Scroll down the page looking in the side column until you see a "+ GOOGLE" button.
4. Click the +GOOGLE button. You'll get two options: You can add the blog feed (it's called the RSS feed) to a gadget on your iGoogle homepage, or you can add it to Google Reader. Click on the "Add to Google homepage" button.

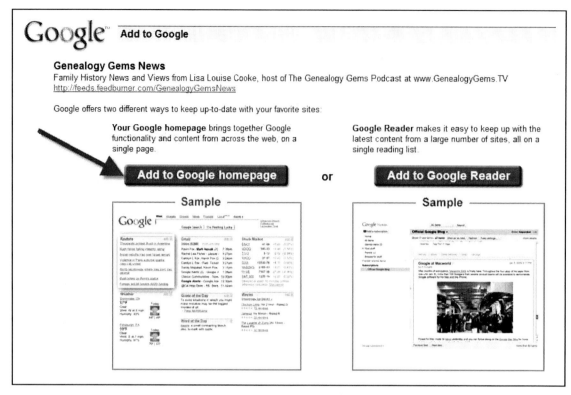

5. You will automatically be sent back to the your iGoogle homepage and there you will see a new gadget in the upper left corner called "Genealogy Gems News". This gadget will contain the three most recent postings on the blog website.
6. To go directly to the blog's website click the gadget title.
7. To learn more about what a blog post is about, hover your mouse over the title of the article.
8. To go directly to a specific blog post: Click the title of the blog post inside the gadget.
9. Every time a blogger or podcaster publishes a new article or episode your gadget will automatically update. This is called "subscribing" even though it is totally free! You are tapping into the "RSS Feed" for the blog or podcast and that's what causes the gadget to update as new articles and episodes are published.

Ongoing education is key to genealogical success. Genealogy blogs and podcasts are a great way to stay up to date on the latest records and search techniques available. Knowing how to set up RSS feed gadgets is going to open all kinds of doors for you.

As with other gadgets, clicking on the gadget title will take you directly to the website. However, you can save that step by accessing blog articles and podcast show notes right from iGoogle. Just click the plus sign next to the left of the episode title to expose the show notes. Use the scroll bar on the right to scroll through the entire page.

You'll notice that when you clicked the plus sign and the article opened, the plus sign turned into a minus sign. When you're done reading and you want to close it up so it's not cluttering your iGoogle homepage, just click the minus sign and it will close back up.

If you decide you want to go ahead and click through to the web page to view it in its entirety, just click on the hyperlinked article or episode title in the gadget.

Many blogs and podcast websites do not have a "+Google" button. But there is a way around that dilemma.

How to Add a Gadget for a Blog Without the +Google Button:

1. Start from the iGoogle tab where you want the gadget to appear
2. Search for or go to the blog you want to add
3. Copy the URL address for the blog's homepage
4. Click the Home button on your browser to return to iGoogle
5. Click the ADD STUFF link
6. In the left hand column click the ADD FEED OR GADGET link next to the orange RSS button
7. Paste the URL address into the box (Make sure you remove **"Error! Hyperlink reference not valid**," which appears in the box)
8. Click the ADD button
9. Click the HOME button to see the gadget on your iGoogle page.

Editing Gadgets

You don't have to take Google Gadgets the way they come. You can edit them and add multiples if that is better suited to you and your research.

In the case of a podcast gadget like the *Genealogy Gems Podcast* gadget you can:
- Change the display
  - Headlines only
  - Headline and lead story
  - Slideshow
- How many episodes appear in the gadget (1-9)

In the case of what are commonly referred to as "desktop gadgets" such as the To Do List and Sticky Note gadgets, you can edit the:
- Title
  - Free form text
- Background Color
  - Black
    - Blue
    - Green
    - Red
    - Pink
    - Orange

- Text Color
  - Same options as background color

How to Edit a Google Gadget:

1. Click the down arrow button in the upper right corner of the gadget to open up the editing menu
2. Select EDIT SETTINGS
3. Make edits
4. Click the SAVE button

You can use this same technique with the To Do List Gadget. You can have multiple to-do lists, each uniquely titled and color-coded.

Organization and Layout

As you can see from the example below, your iGoogle homepage can become full quite quickly. Having a consistent layout and organizational method will help you be able to grab the gadget you need quickly and easily.

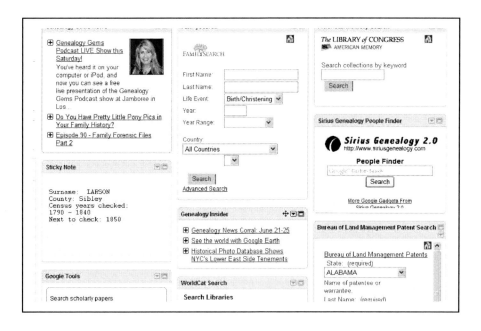

The default layout for iGoogle is three columns. However there are other options.

How to Edit Your iGoogle Layout:

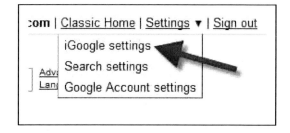

1. Go to your iGoogle homepage
2. Click the SETTINGS link in the upper right corner of the page
3. Select iGOOGLE SETTINGS from the drop down menu

4. Scroll down to the bottom of the page to the layout area
5. Click the radial button for the desired layout

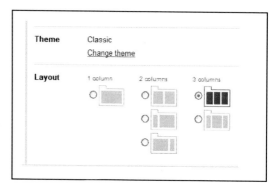

Start by sorting gadgets into columns by type. Then reorganize your gadgets by simply clicking on the title bar of the gadget to grab it and dragging it to the desired location. Feel free to play around with the layout, but here's my recommendation:

- 3 Column Layout
- Left Column: Search Gadgets (Ancestry, FamilySearch, WorldCat, etc.)
- Center Column: Desktop Tool Gadgets (Gmail, to-do lists, etc.)
- Right Column: Educational Gadgets (Podcast, Blogs, Welcome to iGoogle, etc.)
- Most frequently used gadgets at the top, less frequently used gadgets toward the bottom

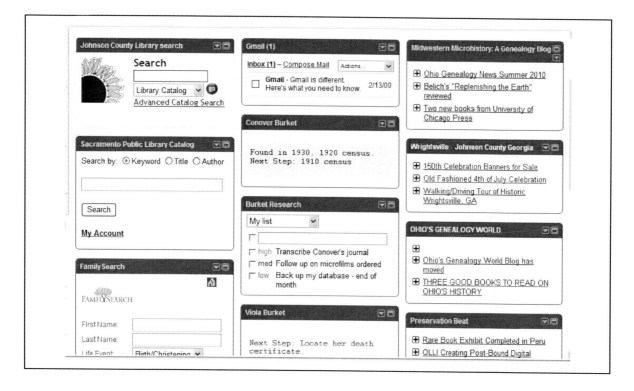

Hide & Seek Storage

Sometimes you'll want lots of gadgets on your page, but some you will use rarely. You can save space by minimizing lesser-used gadgets.

How to Minimize/Maximize a Gadget:

1. Click the down arrow button in the upper right corner of the gadget box
2. Select MINIMIZE THIS GADGET from the drop down menu
3. To restore the gadget to full size, click the down arrow again and select EXPAND THIS GADGET

Spice it up!

Tired of the plain old classic white of Google? Now you can spice up your iGoogle homepage with themes! Themes add not only an image of your choice to the banner across the top of your iGoogle page, but also a complete color scheme to your gadgets and text. There are thousands of ready-made themes to choose from:

Here's an example of one of my favorites called *Spring Scape*:

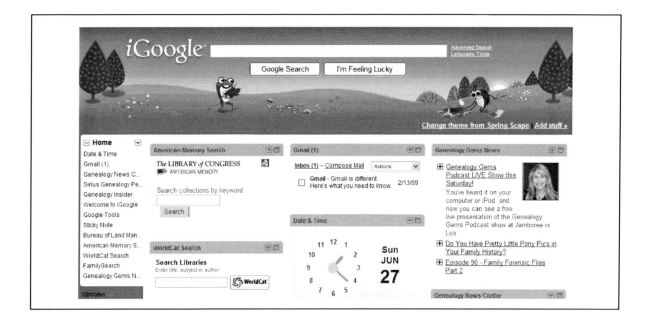

How to Change Your iGoogle Homepage Theme:

1. In the upper right corner click "Select Theme"
2. Click CHANGE THEME FROM CLASSIC link in the upper right corner
3. Click the MORE OPTIONS link on the left
4. Now you are in Google's Themes Gallery. Type keywords in the Search Box to locate themes that interest you.
5. Click the ADD IT NOW button for the theme of your choice.

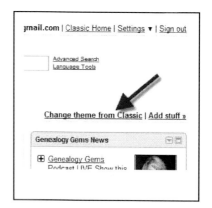

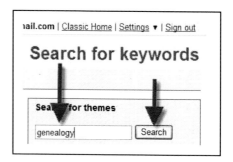

Genealogy Road Rules is a theme I created. It's available in the Google Themes Gallery:

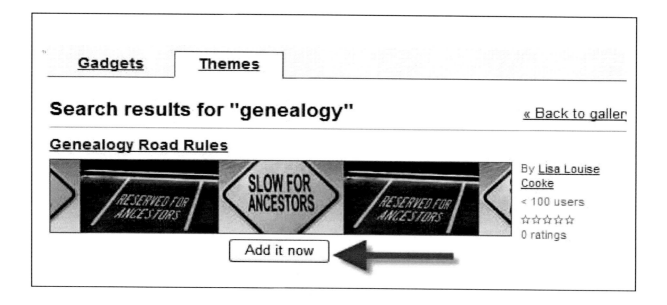

And here's what it looks like on iGoogle:

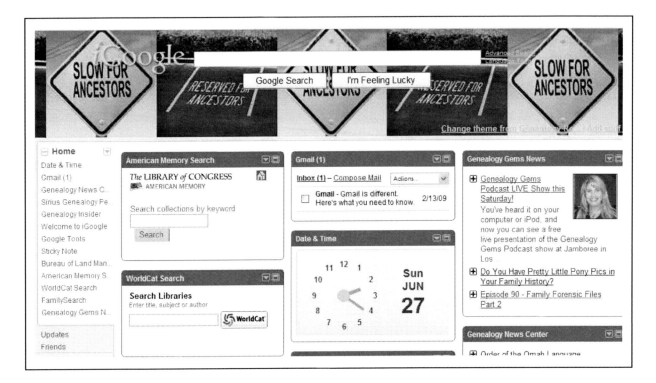

Themes make it just a little more fun to be online. Try one and if you don't like it, you can change it at anytime. Many themes will dynamically change to match your time zone. Just enter your zip code and watch it change throughout the day!

Expand iGoogle With Tabs

Feeling like you need more room? Expand iGoogle with tabs.

Adding a tab to your iGoogle homepage adds an entirely new layer of gadgets and organization. Each tab can be customized to a particular type of work you do on your computer, or a particular area of your genealogy research. For example, you could have a tab for each of the major lines of your family that you are researching and the gadgets on each tab can be unique to that research.

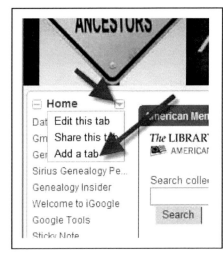

How to Add a Tab to iGoogle:

1. Go to your iGoogle homepage
2. Click the down arrow next to the word Home in the far left column (Home is Tab #1)
3. Select ADD A TAB from the drop down menu
4. In the "Add A Tab" pop up box, type the name of the tab (you can always change it later)

5. Unclick the "I'm feeling lucky" box. If this is left checked iGoogle will automatically add stuff based on tab name
6. Click the OK button on the pop up box
7. You will now have a second tab in the left column and essentially a blank screen to populate with new gadgets pertaining to that tab name.
8. Add gadgets by clicking the LOOK FOR NEW STUFF TO ADD button or by dragging and dropping items from the Home tab onto the new tab.

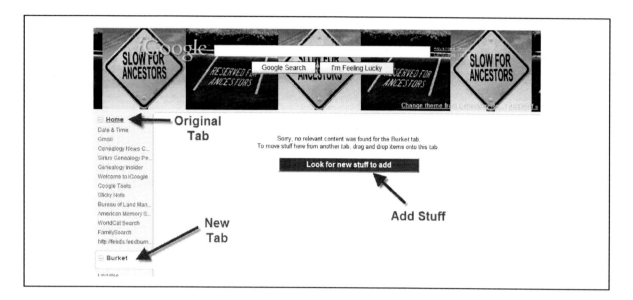

Don't worry, your original tab is still there, it's just behind the new tab. You can switch between the tabs by clicking on the desired tab's name.

Here's an example of a tab that is devoted to the research of a particular surname. The gadgets are all websites, tools, and notes used for that research:

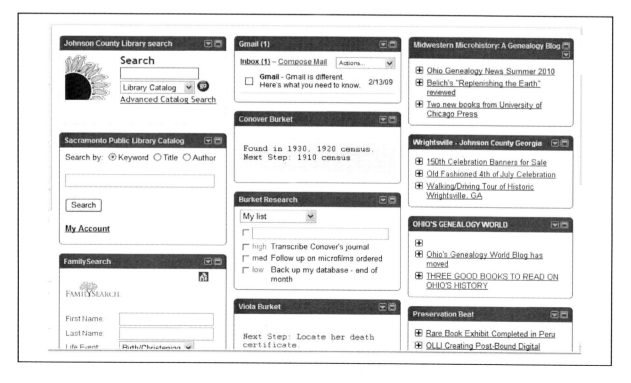

The sticky notes are even color-coded: blue for male ancestors, pink for female ancestors!

When it comes to iGoogle, you can customize to your heart's content to construct a homepage that keeps you organized, focused and ready to start your research day!

CHAPTER 9
Google Books

URL Address: http://books.google.com/

Imagine having access to millions of hard to find and out of print books for free. That's what you get when you use Google Books! This robust tool lends itself particularly well to genealogy research because old, out of copyright books are its specialty. In this chapter you will learn how to locate books about your research topics from the millions available. To get started, watch a quick overview of Google Books with Allison Stacy, Editor & Publisher of *Family Tree Magazine*.

See It In Action!
Video: ***Using Google Books Search***
http://www.youtube.com/watch?v=1R1lgCRln3k

Overview of Google Books

The origin of Google Books goes all the way back to 1996, before Google had become a household word. Graduate computer science students and future Google co-founders Sergey Brin and Larry Page had a shared goal to make digital libraries. They envisioned a future in which vast collections of books would be digitized and "web crawlers" would be used to index the books' content. Computers would be able to analyze the connections between the books, determining their relevance and usefulness by tracking the number and quality of citations from other books.

They eventually developed a web crawler technology that evolved into the PageRank algorithm behind today's Google search. By 2002 a secret "books" project began, which retained the same focus: to digitize all of the books in the world and make them available online.

By 2004 the project was announced as "Google Print" and publishers began partnering with the project. The following year the project's name was changed from Google Print to Google Books. So you could say that Google's roots can be traced back to books. And Google Books has moved to the forefront as a powerful tool for those tracing their roots.

Book Search works just like Google's Web search and delivers the same type of results. Like many of the Google tools, there are advanced search features that can help you narrow your focus and zero in on what you're looking for.

Types of Book Content

While browsing and searching Google Books you will come across four different types of content:

- Public Domain Books – full text and downloadable as PDF file
- Out of Copyright Books – preview and some full text
- In Copyright, with Publisher's Permission Books – preview and some full text
- Magazines

The books and magazines found on Google Books come from two key sources:

- *The Library Project* which includes partnerships with several major libraries
- *The Partner Program* which identifies books through agreements with publishers and authors

Learn more about the Library project from Librarians themselves:
VIDEO: *Google Book Search: UC Library Partnership*
http://www.youtube.com/watch?v=xN0iyzpiZPg

Google takes a partnership approach to acquiring their content, striking agreements to digitize materials under agreed-upon guidelines. However, there has been some controversy over the years as to how books are identified for digitization, how copyright law applies, and what role the actual author plays. Google has sought feedback from its users and works to come to agreements with the various parties and organizations involved. Google Books continues to grow and change. Only time will tell if the goal of digitizing the world's books will be achieved.

Learn more about how Google Books works and the recent settlement agreement between Google and a broad class of authors and publishers. Please note that this agreement resolves a United States lawsuit, and therefore directly affects only those users who access Book Search in the U.S. The following video begins with a review of the various "views" of books, and then around the 3 minute mark discusses the settlement agreement.

VIDEO: *Google Books Settlement Agreement with Authors and Publishers*
http://www.youtube.com/watch?v=UwnbCmVrlSQ

www.GenealogyGems.com

Accessing Content

In every case there will be a "Book Overview" page, including information such as:

- Title
- Author
- Summary paragraph
- Date of publication
- Book length
- "Where to Buy and Borrow" Links

Some books may also have:

- Reviews
- Related Books list
- Common terms and phrases
- Scholarly and Web page references
- A map showing places mentioned in the book
- Popular passages from the book
- Table of Contents or Chapter Titles
- Other editions
- ISBN number

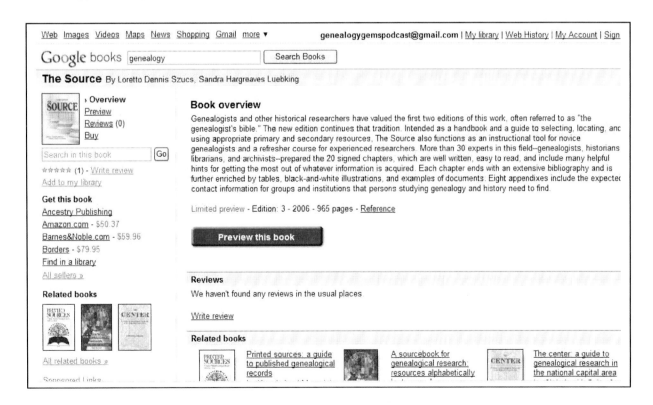

The Book Overview, previously known as the "About This Book" page continues to be expanded as agreements are reached and data is collected by Google.

There are four different types of views available in Google Books Search:

View: **Full**
Availability: copyright books or if agreement has been reached with the publisher or author
Pages: All pages are viewable
Download: Yes as PDF if in the Public Domain

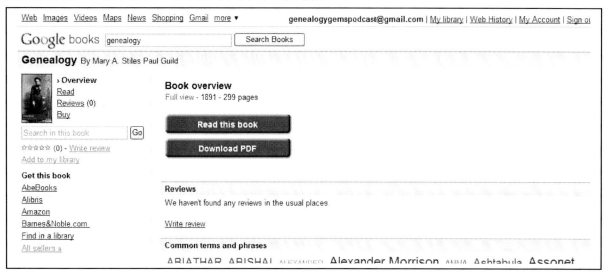

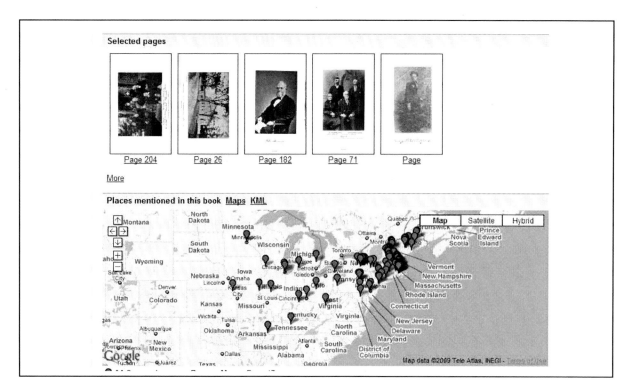

View: **Limited Preview**
Availability: If agreement has been reached with the publisher or author
Pages: Some pages are viewable
Download: No

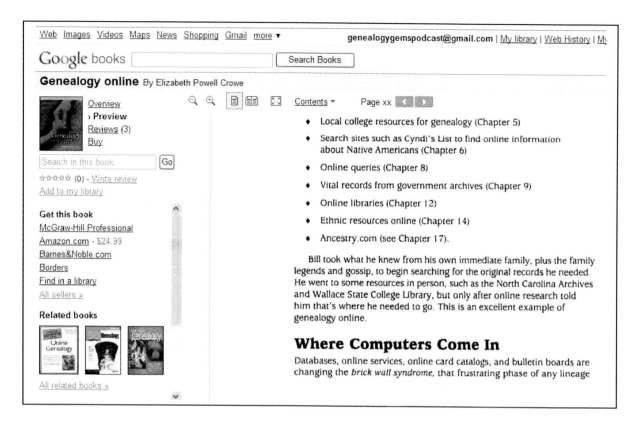

View: **Snippet**
Availability: Some of the remaining books not covered by full view or preview
Pages: No pages are viewable. Only a very small amount of text showing your search terms in context is provided.
Download: No

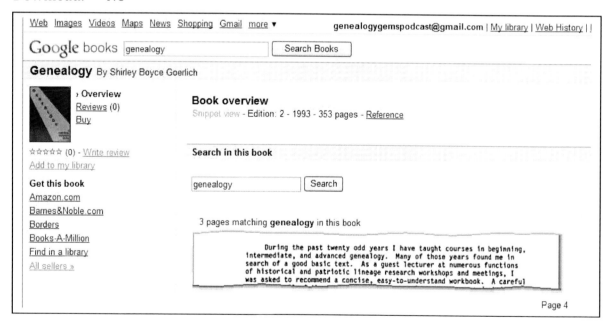

View: **No Preview Available**
Availability: All other remaining books
Pages: No pages are viewable.
Download: No

A Sample Search

As you can imagine, there is a wealth of genealogical and historical information in the hundreds of thousands of volumes listed in Google Books. Let's do a sample search to explore the methods of locating and using these materials.

While you don't need to be signed in to your Google account in order to do a search, doing so will ensure that you have full usage of all the available features of Book Search. From the Google Books home page at http://books.google.com/ click the "Sign In" link in the upper right corner. This will take you to your Google accounts page where you will enter your email address and password, and then click the Sign-In Button.

Now you are signed in and back on the Google Books home page ready to search. The first step is to define our search parameters:

Example:
Surnames: Paulus, Chenoweth, and Burket
Where: Randolph County, Indiana
Timeframe: 19th century

Because old county histories are usually out of copyright and in the public domain we have a very good chance of locating the right volume and having full view access to it. We start by typing our search terms *Randolph County Indiana History* into the search box and clicking the Book Search button.

There are two key items to notice on the results page and they appear in the light blue bar across the top.

Notice first (on the left) that the "Showing" results are drawing from "All Books" (Note: While working in Google Books, keep in mind that when the term "Book" is used it typically includes all content including magazines.) Very often your results list will be quite long and you may elect to start by viewing books that offer the free Full View or Limited Preview. To do that, simply click the drop down menu, make your selection, and Google will automatically run a new search.

The second thing you will notice on the right side of the light blue bar is the total number of results that your search delivered. At the time of this writing, this search delivered over 2,500 results. Seeing the total results number will help you determine how much further you will want to narrow your search. The Advanced Search is just the place to do that.

Google Books Advanced Search

To conduct an advanced search, click the "Advanced Search" link just to the right of the Search Books button at the top of the page. You can use the same search operators in the blue area at the top of the page such as:

- "+" Plus operator which ensures that common words, numbers, and letters that Google search often ignores are included
  (e.g. charles +de gaulle)

- "-" Minus operator excludes all articles with the associated word or phrase
  (e.g. hoover –edgar)

- Phrase search in quotation marks returns only the exact phrase
  (e.g. "state of liberty")

- "OR" operator giving you word options
  (e.g. county or parish)

Other features for narrowing your search include:
- View selection
- Content type selection
- Language

As well as some options unique to books such as searching by:
- Title
- Author
- Publisher
- Subject
- Publication Date
- ISBN
- ISSN

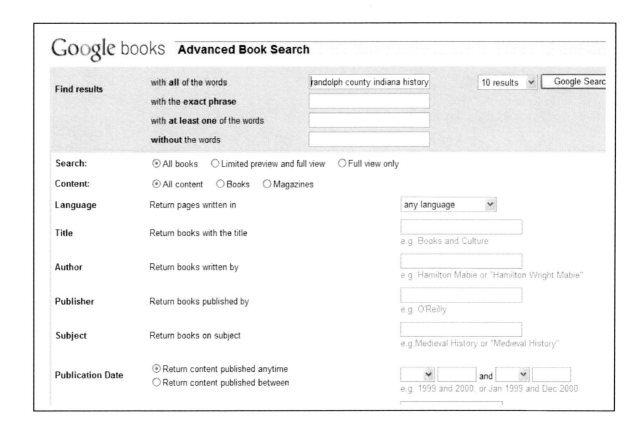

To narrow our sample search there are a couple of selections we can make. In the "with at least one of the words" field we can enter our surnames: Burket Chenoweth Paulus, which is like telling Google Books to return results for our original search terms and at least one of those surnames.

We can also select the "Books Only" button. Then in the Publication Date fields we can select "Return content published between" and enter the years 1800 and 1900. Here are the results of our advanced search:

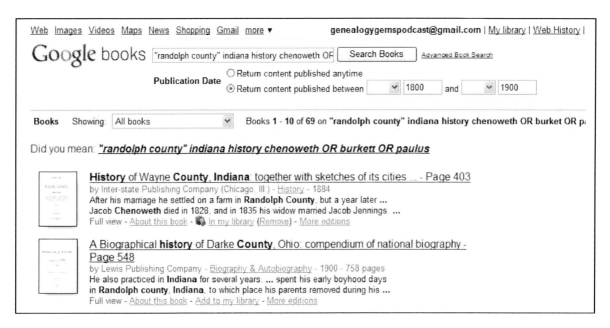

www.GenealogyGems.com

Now we are down to just over 100 books. A quick glance of the results reveals that the word county may be throwing our results off just a bit, particularly since "Randolph" can be a person's name as well. By adding quotation marks around "Randolph County" in the search field and rerunning the search we should get even better results.

This search delivers a manageable number of books to be reviewed. *The History of Wayne County* looks promising. This is an example of the power of the Book Search. If you were searching in a traditional library, you would naturally be pulling books off the shelf with "Randolph County" in their title. However, Google Books reveals that people with the surnames we are looking for who hailed from Randolph County also appear in neighboring county history books!

Click on the title to access the book.

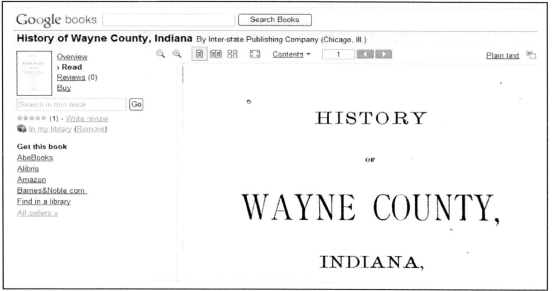

The page viewer offers many familiar options for interacting with the digitized pages of this book. Across the top you will see icons for:

- Zoom
- One and two page views
- Thumbnail view
- Full Screen
- Table of Contents drop down menu
- Page number search box
- Left and right page scroll buttons

In addition you will also find some great tools for utilizing the images:

Plain Text Converter: Clicking this button will convert the digitized page to plain text, which gives you the flexibility to highlight, copy, and paste portions of the text. Here's an example of text that I was able to copy and paste from the plain text view:

> *"The town now has three stores—one, a general store, kept by Nathan Grave; two groceries, by Wm. Robinson and Hiram Surplice. The practicing physicians are: Drs. Wm. Williams, James Courtney and W. T. Griffiths. Blacksmiths: Thomas White, Hiram Gist, A. Jackson. Chair- maker, Charles Wolverton. The town has two churches, Methodist and Disciples, and lodges of Odd Fellows and Masons."*

While in Plain Text view you have the ability to download the plain text version of the book as a PDF document to your computer. To return to the digitized page click the Page Images link in the upper right corner.

Clip Tool: This tool gives you incredible flexibility for using and sharing portions of the book. Simply click the Clip Tool icon and your cursor will become a plus sign. Place the plus cursor in the upper left corner of the section you want to clip and click and drag the cursor to create a box around the text. A clip window will automatically pop up giving you the following options:

> ***Selection Text*** – this can be highlighted, copied, and pasted in other documents. By clicking the "Translate" link, it can also be translated into other languages. (Application Example: You are researching your German ancestors and have located a book written in German. You can select portions and automatically translate them.)

> ***Image*** – the clipped text now resides in Google and the image of the clip can be linked to with the URL address provided in the clip box.

> ***Embed*** – If you have a web site or family history blog you can quickly and easily share your findings online. The clip tool automatically generates the HTML code you will need to include your clipped text on your web pages. Just highlight, copy, and paste the code.

Link Tool: This tool allows you to email or instant message a link that will take the recipient directly to the book and the page that you are currently working with. (Application Example: Another researcher across the country is collaborating with you. You can instantly send your newest discovery to them.)

PDF Document Download Tool: You can open or save both the digital and the plain text versions of the book to your computer hard drive the entire book in PDF format for future reference.

Search Within the Book

To search further within this book just type keywords into the search box in the column on the left side of the page and click the Go button. For example, you can enter an additional surname you are interested in. In this example, searching on the name Lightner instantly reveals one occurrence of the name on page 498.

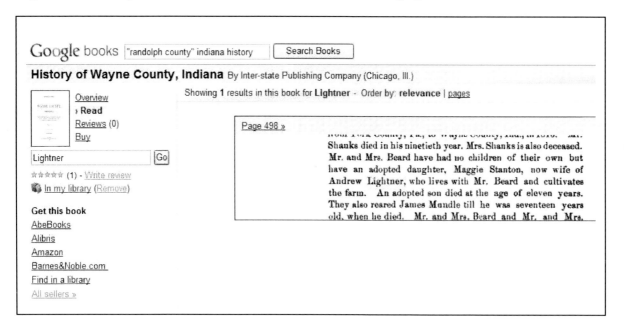

The example of identifying another surname and searching for it within the text points us toward another powerful tool within Google Books. It's called MyLibrary, and it allows you to create a virtual library within Google Books of the books you have found. To get to MyLibrary just click the MyLibrary link found at the top of every page within Google Books.

Here you can:

- Create a MyLibrary profile
- Import books from your searches into MyLibrary for future reference
- Export MyLibrary as an XML document
- View your books in list or cover view
- Rate each book with a 5 star rating system according to their value to your research
- Add notes to each book
- Add labels to each book (Application Example: Surnames, locations, and other genealogical topics of interest)
- Write a review of the book for the benefit of all researchers

Image Above: Example of MyLibrary

Keys to Success

1. *Be aware and keep in mind that Book Search isn't perfect.* Some pages are not high quality and using the search feature will not always pick up your search terms. In the end it comes down to using your best judgment. For example, I have viewed the microfilm version of the Randolph County, Indiana County History of by E. Tucker, and yet it did not come up in the advanced search results. This was because the search didn't detect the surnames that were added in the advanced search, even though I have located all three surnames in the microfilmed version of the text. The key to success is to try a variety of advanced searches, and if you don't see a book that you would expect to find, try a title or author search to pull it up individually.

2. Take full advantage of the MyLibrary feature and keep records of what you've searched. Book Search is vast so keeping notes as you search will help avoid duplication of effort and ensure you get the most out of your time spent.

3. Utilize the Advanced Search and try your searches from many different angles. Search is not an exact science and takes some trial and error.

4. Learn from fellow genealogists about how they use Google Books.
   VIDEO: *Google Book Search: Researching Your (Ancestral Roots)*
   http://www.youtube.com/watch?v=UwnbCmVrISQ

CHAPTER 10
Google News Timeline

URL Address: http://www.google.com/archivesearch

Newspapers are one of the most interesting and diverse genealogical resources available. While there are several web sites that require paid subscription on the Internet, free access to newspapers is also growing. The Google News Archive and Timeline is at the top of that list and is a great place to begin before you start pulling out your credit card for subscription websites.

Overview of Google News Archive

Google's News Archive search provides an easy way to search and explore historical newspaper archives. You can perform a search on any topic applicable to your genealogy research in two types of online content. Here are just some of the possible search topics that could provide greater insight into your family tree:

- Family surnames
- Family businesses
- Employers your ancestors worked for
- Schools your ancestors attended
- Clubs and activities in which your ancestors participated
- Vital Record Notices – births, marriages, divorces, deaths
- Events that occurred in your ancestor's community while they lived there
- World events that occurred during your ancestor's lifetime

Anything that might have made the news is something worth searching for in the Google News Archive.

Types of Content

There are a couple of different types of content that you will find in the News Archive.

The first type is **_partner content_** digitized by Google through their News Archive Partner Program. Google partners with publishers and repositories to make their newspaper holdings available as part of the News Archive search. If the content has already been digitized and is online, Google indexes it and makes it available.

If the content has not been digitized, Google then works with the copyright holder to digitize it and make it full-text searchable online. When you click on a News Archive Partner Program item, you will be taken to a Google-hosted page containing the article within the newspaper page.

Image Right :
full-text searchable
partner content

The second type of content is **online archival materials** that Google has "crawled." News Archive content is mixed together with other articles found all over the Internet. You can determine if the article is part of the News Archive by looking at the details listed beneath the search results. The details will include the newspaper's name followed by "Google News archive."

The third type of content that will appear in your search results is **pay-per-view**, which requires a fee to access. While this is not free content, it does give you a broader picture of what your available online digital content options are.

As I've mentioned, newsworthy events that occurred in your ancestor's community at the time they lived there are great topics to search and learn more about. For instance, if your ancestor was living in San Francisco during or around the time of the Great Earthquake of 1906 you may want to search the News Archive for related articles. Here are examples of the type of results we've discussed:

Search: *The San Francisco Earthquake 1906*

1. News Archive Partner Content (indexed or digitized)
   Result: *The San Francisco Earthquake*, The Sydney Morning Herald, June 19, 1906, Page: 2

2. Online Archival Materials (crawled and catalogued by Google)
   Result: *Literary Women in the San Francisco Earthquake*, The New York Times, May 12, 1906, Page: BR311

3. Pay-Per-View Content (requiring a fee to access)
   Result: *The San Francisco Earthquake*, Los Angeles Times, May 24, 2906 Page: 114

The Timeline Feature

In addition to searching for the most relevant articles for your search terms, the Google News Archive offers a Timeline feature that delivers relevant articles to you organized by date. You can also see a historical overview of the search results by browsing the interactive timeline with the click of a button. The Timeline offers flexibility – you can view timelines showing a century worth of articles down to a month's worth of articles, all organized in date order.

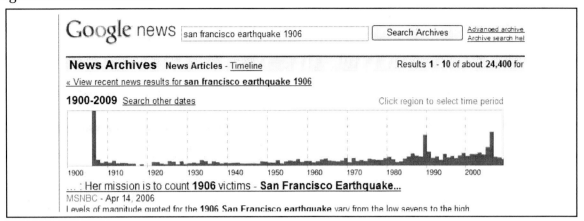

A Sample Search

http://news.google.com/archivesearch

These Google sites may appear simple and unassuming, but there's plenty to work with here. Before you begin, be sure that you're signed into your Google account.

The Family History Scenario

I am interested in learning more about the early years of the automobile. The great grandfather I am researching was the head blacksmith (and later auto manager) for a prominent landowner in England, who owned the very first horseless carriage in England just before the turn of the 20th century. Family journals provide the name of the landowner, Sir David Salomon, and allude to events in those early automotive days. With the advent of such an exciting new machine in Britain (referred to in the journals as a "horseless carriage"), I'm guessing there may have been newspaper articles written about the activities in which Sir David and great grandfather participated.

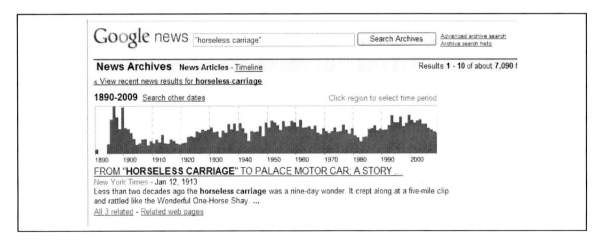

Search Criteria

I enter the term "horseless carriage" and click the SEARCH ARCHIVE button.

Search Results

The results returned cover the years 1890 – current day and amount to 7,000, so I want to narrow down my search. There are a couple of key words I can use to do that:

- "Exhibition" because I have a photo of the first horseless carriage exhibition that my great grandfather attended
- "England" to narrow it down by country
- Salomon, the name of great grandfather's employer

I'm going to try "Exhibition" because it was mentioned specifically in the family journals. In the search box I will add a "+" and the word "Exhibition" and click the Search Archives button. This refined search is successful in narrowing down the results to 306.

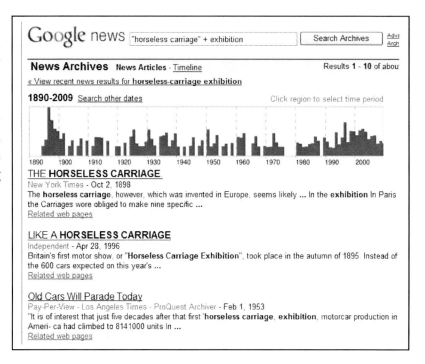

Focusing Further: Incorporating the Timeline into the Search

I am really looking for stories prior to 1912 when great grandfather immigrated to America. A specific decade can be viewed by clicking on the decade section on the timeline (ex. 1890), or specific years can be viewed by clicking the "Search other dates" link above the timeline. Clicking the link will reveal fields where you can type specific dates such as 1890 to 1912. With a click of the Go button the timeline now transforms into a timeline representing 1890 to 1912.

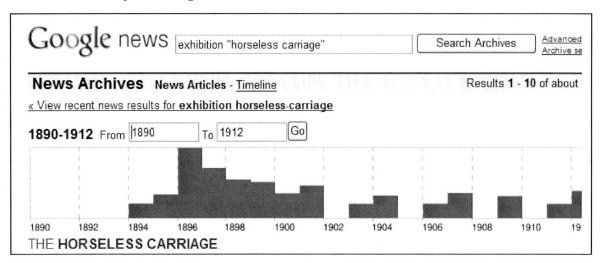

The bars on the timeline represent the number of articles available from those particular years. The higher the bar, the more plentiful the articles. Many of these articles provide a wealth of information about the early years of the automobile. However, if I want to find an article that specifically names "Salomon" or "Tunbridge Wells" where the exhibition would have taken place, additional criteria must be added to my search. So in the search box I will add a "+" and the word "Tunbridge."

The first thing to notice is that the date range has changed. Google News Archive was unable to find any articles in my specified range of 1890 – 1912, so it conducted a search automatically through all available years, and surprisingly it found results. This is an important reminder that when searching newspapers, it can actually hinder your research to limit your search to specific years. Many important and noteworthy events and people are written about long after they have passed, as is the case in this scenario.

The first article, though written as recently as 1996, certainly stands out as a possible goldmine of information. Each article listed in the results will include an abstract or "snippet" of the text. This abstract sounds very promising as it not only includes my search terms but asks the question I've been wondering about: "Why did Tunbridge Wells find itself the home of state-of-the-art motoring?"

This article (an example of *Online Archival Materials content*) is an absolute gem! Up until now all I've had is a very brief mention of the exhibition in great grandfather's autobiography and a photo of the exhibition on Ebay of him standing off to the side of the horseless carriage carrying Sir David Salomon. Now, thanks to the Google News Archive, I have a wealth of background information! And this is just the first article!

www.GenealogyGems.com

Image Above: Linked article from 1996 referring to "horseless carriage."

Click the Back button to return to the results list.

The third article in the list called "Emancipation Day" also catches the eye. Written in 1926, the article abstract indicates that it may provide a first hand account of the exhibition. "I drove my car to the exhibition grounds very early in the morning..." Clicking on the article title brings up the article within the context of the actual newspaper page it appeared on within the Google News Viewer. This is an example of partner content that was scanned and made available by Google.

The viewer has many of the same features you have probably found in other online digital content viewers, including:

- Zoom in and out
- Full Screen view
- Page browsing
- Related Articles list
- Grab handle browsing
- Full page snippet view

Image Above: The Google News viewer showing the "Emancipation Day" article

This article not only includes a first hand account of the exhibition, but also a photograph of Sr. David Salomon in his automobile workshop – the workshop where great grandfather was sure to have worked according to his journal.

Advanced Archive Search

In addition to the Timeline, Google News Archives offers an Advanced Search to assist you in focusing in on the articles and information you are looking for. A link to Advanced Archive Search can be found on the Google News Archive homepage as well as on all search results pages to the right of the search box and Show Timeline button.

Image Above: Google Advanced News Archive Search page.

By adding "operators" that further define your search terms, you can increase your search success within the News Archive. You can specify:

- Words and phrases you want included or omitted
- Dates – exact dates, month and year, or year

  SEARCH TIP: To restrict all articles before a given date, leave the "from" date blank, and after a given date by leaving the "to" date blank.

- Language of the text
- Source (e.g. New York Times)

  SEARCH TIP: Try entering "Google News Archive" to see only free News Archive content.

- The price you are willing to pay for pay-per-view content

  SEARCH TIP: Clicking on pay-per-view results does not incur a cost and will usually allow you to see a limited preview of the article.

You can also select the way you want to view the results. At the top of the page you can select how many articles will be listed per page of results. At the bottom you can choose to view articles, the full timeline, and the news timeline. Try selecting each of these options and running your search to explore the full range of available content.

The News Archive search works much the same way as Google Web search. This means you can use many of the same operators such as:

- "Site" operator
  (e.g. site:nytimes.com State of Liberty)

- "+" Plus operator which ensures that common words, numbers and letters that Google search often ignores are included
  (e.g. charles +de gaulle)

- "-" Minus operator excludes all articles with the associated word or phrase
  (e.g. hoover –edgar)

- Phrase search in quotation marks returns only the exact phrase
  (e.g. "state of liberty")

- "OR" operator giving you word options
  (e.g. county or parish)

Keys to Success

There are several keys to successful News Archive searches:

1. Develop a list of keywords, phrases, and dates that will help you focus your search.

2. Keep a record of what you've searched. The News Archive is vast and keeping notes as you search will help you avoid duplication or missing a key article.

3. Take advantage of Advanced Search.

4. Utilize the Timeline. Being able to see your search within a timeframe context may provide additional clues and ideas. The timeline also offers a flexible search alternative.

5. Don't hesitate to click through to view the abstracts of pay-per-view articles. You may find usable information, or enough reason to purchase a particular article.

CHAPTER 11
Google Translate, Translation Toolkit
& Google Script Converter

http://translate.google.com

Chances are at some point in your research you will find yourself needing to do some translation – whether it be a website, book, or letter. More than once I've come across a website that mentions an unusual surname that I'm working on but it's in German or some other language. This is where translation websites like Google Translate can really come in handy. Even if they don't do a perfect job of translating they will be able to give you the general idea of what the text says.

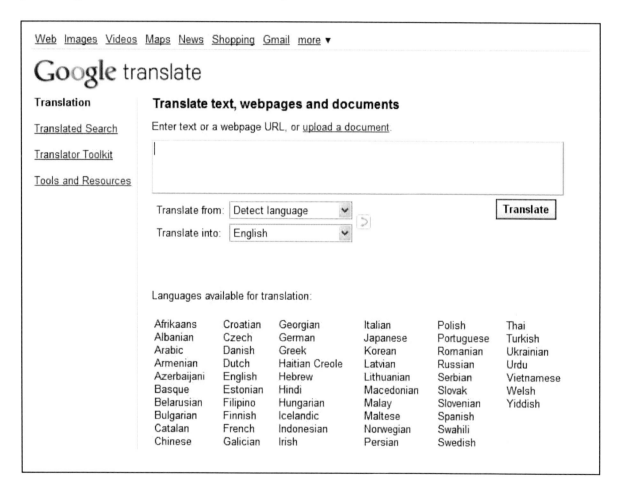

There are currently over 50 languages available for translation and Google adds new ones regularly.

Using Google Translate

Google Translate has come a long way since it was first introduced in October of 2007. In the past the only option was to copy and paste the text to be translated into the text box. As of this writing you have the option to translate:

- Text
- Webpages
- Documents

How to Translate Text:

1. Highlight the text from any web page or document on your computer and copy OR type the text directly into the box
2. Paste the text into the translation box
3. Select the language of the text entered into the box from the "Translate From" drop down menu
4. Select the language you want to translate the text into from the "Translate Into" drop down menu
5. The translation will automatically appear

Here's an example of Great Grandmother's recipe in German translated with Google Translate:

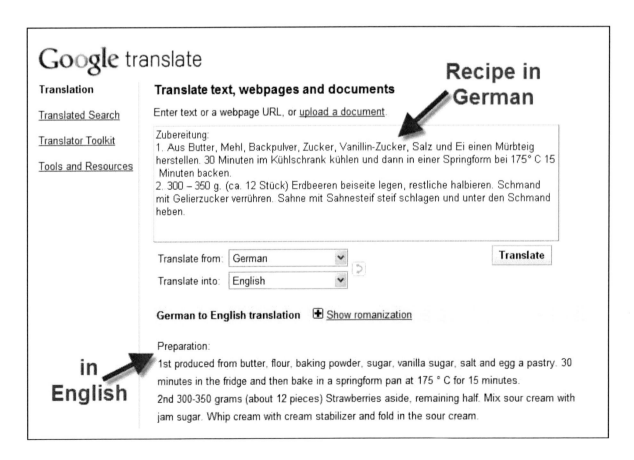

See It For Yourself:
VIDEO: *Text Translation on Google Translate*
http://www.youtube.com/watch?v=FijOWfO3Frk&feature=channel

How to Translate a Web Page:

1. Go to the web page you want to translate
2. Highlight the web page URL address and copy
3. Go to http://translate.google.com
4. Paste the URL address into the translation box

5. Select the language of the text entered into the box from the "Translate From" drop down menu
6. Select the language you want to translate the text into from the "Translate Into" drop down menu
7. Click the TRANSLATE button

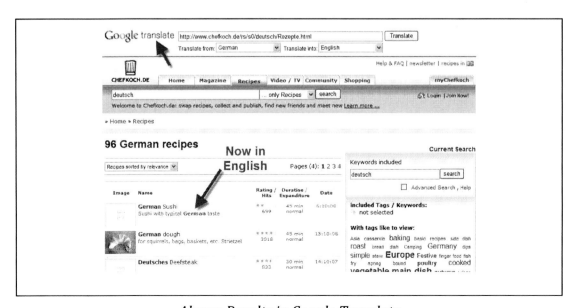

Above: Results in Google Translate.

How to Translate a Document:

1. Go to
   http://translate.google.com
2. Click the UPLOAD A
   DOCUMENT link
3. Click the BROWSE button
4. In the pop up window locate
   the document you want to
   translate on your computer
   hard drive
5. Click OPEN

6. Select the language of the text entered into the box from the "Translate From" drop
   down menu
7. Select the language you want to translate the text into from the "Translate Into"
   drop down menu
8. Click the TRANSLATE button.

The translated document will appear on your screen.

Pronunciation

Another great new feature of Google Translate is the "Listen to this Translation" button.
When translating small amounts of text the "Listen to" button will appear next to the
translated words.

If you have speakers or a headset plugged into your computer you will be able to hear the word being pronounced in the translated language.

Cross Language Search

A genealogist knows that it is critical to consult maps of the time period being researched because borders often change. Along with border changes come language changes. For example, you may be researching German ancestors and have documents written in German, but you should consult with a Polish or Russian archive for assistance. Cross Language Search allows you to perform searches between any two languages supported by Google Translate. The translation process is the same. Simply select the desired languages from the Translate From and Translate Into drop down menus.

Unknown Languages

Occasionally genealogists come across languages they don't recognize in books, documents, or websites. Using Google's Detect Language feature makes it a snap to identify an unknown language.

How to Detect A Language:

1. Go to http://translate.google.com
2. Type or copy and paste the text or URL address into the translation box
3. Select DETECT LANGUAGE from the "Translate From" drop down menu
4. Google Translate will automatically indicate in the TRANSLATE FROM field which language has been detected
5. Select the desired language in the TRANSLATE INTO box
6. Click the TRANSLATE button (For small amounts of text Google will automatically translate)

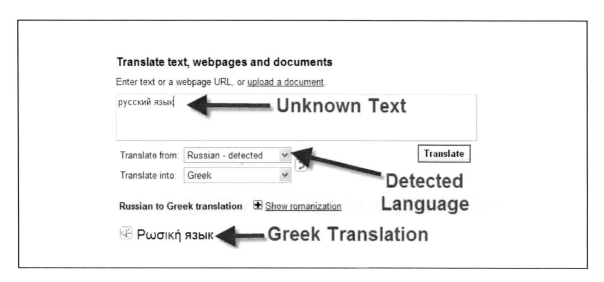

Going Global

Let's say you have a blog or website about your family tree and you have a lot of Germans, or Italians, or Russians, etc. that you're researching and talking about. By incorporating Google Translate into your website or blog, you can make it accessible to researchers and distant cousins who do not speak English. Think how much more far-reaching this will make your website and how it may facilitate being able to make connections!

By adding the Translate gadget to your web page, you can offer instant access to automatic translations of that page. Adding the gadget is quick and easy. It will also include all of the new languages recently added.

How to Add Google Translator to Your Web Pages:

1. Go to the Google Translate Tools and Resources page at http://translate.google.com/translate_tools
2. Select the language of your web page
3. Select either ALL LANGUAGES or select specific languages

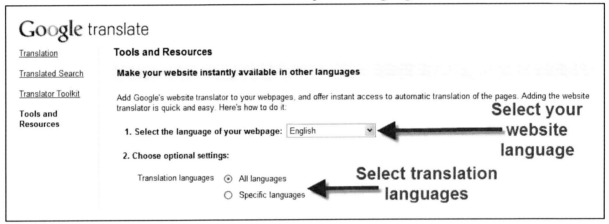

4. Copy the HTML code automatically generated by Google
5. Click the PREVIEW AND TRY button to see how the code will appear on your website
6. Paste the code into your website
7. Publish

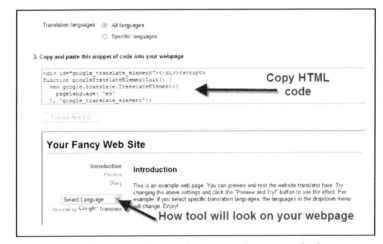

On the Google Translate Tools and Resources page you can also download the free Google Toolbar and add specific translation buttons for one-click access for languages you regularly deal with in your research.

114   www.GenealogyGems.com

How to Add the Google Translate Gadget to Your iGoogle Homepage:

1. Go to your iGoogle homepage
2. Click the Add Stuff Link
3. Type Google Translate in the Search box
4. Click the ADD IT NOW for the Google Translate gadget
5. Click the HOME button to go back to your iGoogle homepage where you will find the gadget in the upper left corner
6. Drag and drop the gadget to the desired location

Google Translator Toolkit

Google Translator Toolkit was designed to help translators more quickly and efficiently through one shared translation platform. It's different from Google Translate because Google Translate provides "automatic translations" produced solely by technology, without human translator intervention. By comparison, Google Translator Toolkit allows actual translators to work faster and more accurately with the aid of technology like Google Translate.

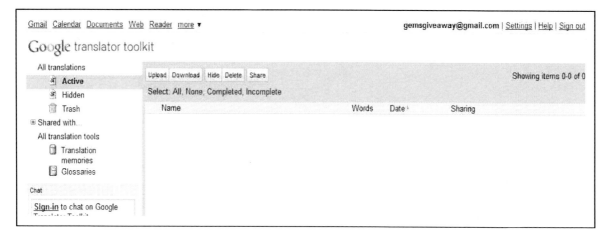

While Google Translator Toolkit may not be something you need right now, it's good to be aware that you can:

- Upload Word documents, OpenOffice, RTF, HTML, text, Wikipedia articles and Knols.

- Use previous human translations and machine translation to "pre-translate" your uploaded documents.
- Use Google's simple WYSIWYG editor to improve the pre-translation
- Invite others (via email) to edit or view your translations
- Download documents to your desktop in their native formats (i.e. Word, OpenOffice, RTF, or HTML)
- Publish your Wikipedia and Knol translations back to Wikipedia or Knol.

To learn more about how the Translator Tool Kit works...
VIDEO: *Translator Tool Kit*
http://www.youtube.com/watch?v=C7W2NJFdoIg

Google Script Converter

When Google is working on a new tool but is still fine-tuning it, they don't publicly launch it. Rather, the tool is beta-tested in Google Labs. http://www.googlelabs.com/ One of the up and coming Google Tools that can be found at Google Labs is called Script Converter.

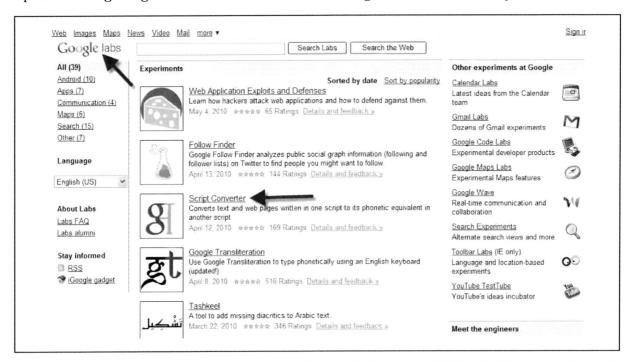

Go to http://scriptconv.googlelabs.com/ and click on script converter.

Type text or a URL address into the text box. Script Converter will automatically detect it and convert it into the desired language script.

Here is my website converted into Hindi script:

The Script Converter currently supports the following scripts:

- Bengali
- Greek
- English
- Persian
- Gujarati
- Devanagari Hindi, Marathi, Nepali)
- Kannada

- Malayalam
- Punjabi
- Russian
- Sanskrit
- Serbian
- Tamil
- Telugu
- Urdu

Notice that the "Genealogy Gems" banner across the top did not convert. If the text on the original page is an image, as in this case, it will not be converted. Also, if the text was not originally present on the page, but rather injected by JavaScript, it will not be converted.

Again this may not be something you use every day, but when you do come across a situation where you need to convert script, tap into the Google Script Converter.

Just for Fun

Here's a language that you don't find every day in your research: Pig Latin!

How to Convert Google Search to Pig Latin:

1. Go to www.google.com
2. Type xx- pig Latin (note the space after the minus sign!)
3. Click the I'M FEELING LUCKY button

A Few Quick Tricks for Research Trip Planning

If you are fortunate enough to be able to take a trip to the land of your ancestor's, or if you need to send an overseas archive payment for services rendered, Google can help you determine the currency type as well as the conversion rate.

Not sure what the currency is used in Romania? Go to Google.com and type in the search box:

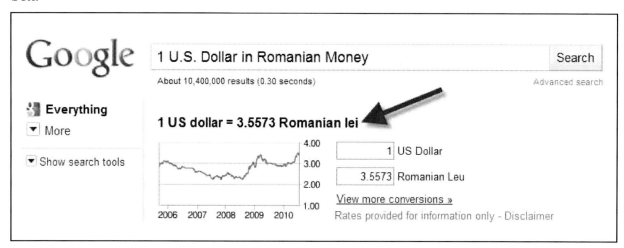

1 U.S. Dollar in Romanian Money

See Money Conversion in Action:
VIDEO: *How to Convert Currency Using Google*
http://www.youtube.com/watch?v=hx0hBfCFRFo

Need to know what the weather will be like for your trip to an ancestral castle in Scotland? Type:

WEATHER EH2 2 (the postal code)

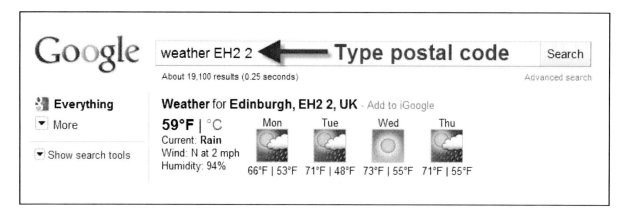

Just a few quick tricks for making your research trip planning a little easier!

CHAPTER 12
YouTube & Google Videos

YouTube was founded in February 2005 and by July 2006 announced it was serving up 100 million videos per day to its users. Shortly thereafter in November, Google purchased YouTube and it remains the world's most popular online video channel.

YouTube is best known for its quirky and funny user uploaded videos. But much like iTunes, it's not just for teenagers anymore. Amidst those millions if not billions of videos hosted on the YouTube web site are a number of videos that would be very useful to the genealogist on several levels.

A search on the word "genealogy" in YouTube results in over 3,400 videos. And "family history" generated about 3,100. So there's a lot to choose from and the number is growing every day.

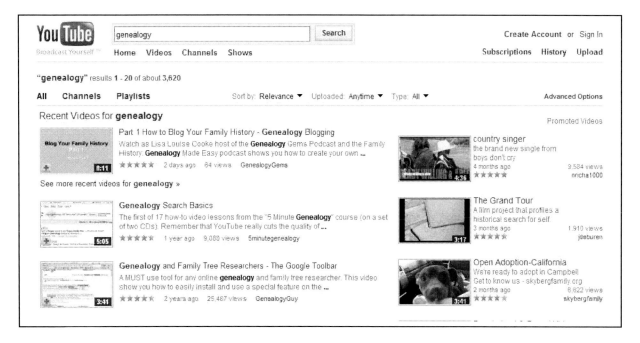

When browsing and searching YouTube keep your eye out for videos that can help you in your research by providing:

- Original vintage footage of events all the way back to the invention of the movie camera

- Family History documentaries created by users that may include your family

- Instructional videos that will help you become a better researcher, create a family heirloom, or learn the latest genealogy software

www.GenealogyGems.com

- Video tours of archives, libraries, and other repositories that will help you prepare for and get the most out of your visit

- Interviews with genealogy experts and vendors

- Entertaining videos that add enjoyment to one of the world's most popular hobbies

Concentrate on the Search

YouTube offers the following browse buttons:
- Videos
- Shows
- Channels

But because YouTube is geared to the entertainment-focused user, avoid browsing the buttons and concentrate on the search box. That's your best tool for finding genealogy-themed videos.

Before we go further, a word about YouTube content: YouTube does have specific Terms of Use rules and attempts to enforce them as best they can when dealing with millions of videos. They rely on the YouTube user community to assist them in flagging and removing inappropriate content.

By following the search suggestions laid out in this chapter, you won't very likely run into objectionable content. But if you do there is a way to "flag" it to alert YouTube so they can take action to remove it if deemed inappropriate.

Watch this quick video to learn how to flag content that violates YouTube's guidelines and help keep YouTube a safe surfing environment.

VIDEO: *Flagging on YouTube: The Basics*
http://www.youtube.com/watch?v=ZA22WSVlCZ4&feature=channel_page

Search YouTube by typing keywords and phrases into the search box and click the Search button. Once you have conducted an initial search, the Advanced Options will then become available to you. You will find the "Advanced Options" link on the right side of the menu bar across the top of the page. Click it and an Advanced Search box will drop down giving you many more options to work with.

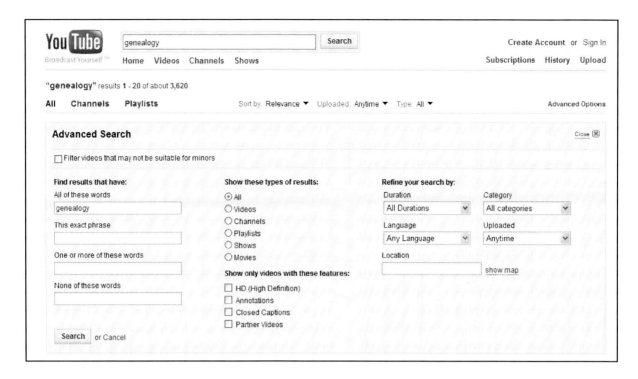

Your first option is a check box that will filter videos that have been identified as inappropriate for minors, even though they are not technically considered in violation of the Terms of Use Guidelines. This would be similar to an "R" rating at the movies.

You will also find four search files offering you the option to find results that have:
- All of these words
- This exact phrase
- One or more of these words
- None of these words

You can also use standard operators referred to in the previous two lessons to further define your search.

There are also radial buttons that allow you to select the type of content you want in the results:

- **All**: all types of content

- **Videos**: videos only

- **Channels**: these are like mini websites within YouTube created by a single video producer, such as my own *Genealogy Gems YouTube Channel* at http://www.youtube.com/GenealogyGems
  To date there are just over 70 channels tagged with the word "genealogy."

- **Playlists**: a playlist is a collection of videos grouped by one user that can be shared among other users with similar interests. There are currently over 2,000 genealogy-tagged user playlists.

- **Shows**: YouTube partners with television shows and video producers to deliver content in a series format. There are no genealogy tagged shows at the time of this writing.

- **Movies**: Full-length movies and trailers are available on YouTube. There were no genealogy tagged movies at the time of this writing.

You can also select videos specifically with the following features:

- High Definition
- Annotations
- Closed Captions
- Partner Videos (such as television studios)

And finally you can refine you search by:

- **Duration**: Options include less than 4 minutes, 4-20 minutes, or longer than 20 minutes

- **Location**: Type in the location or use the map (Application Example: this could be a useful tool for homing in on ancestral hometowns and counties)

- **Category**: There are a limited number of categories and they likely won't help you in locating genealogy related videos

- **Uploaded**: Options include anytime, this month, this week, or today. This can help you locate newly uploaded videos without having to wade through all of them.

Just above the Advanced Search box you will also find a drop down menu called "Sort By" that allows you to sort the results list by:

- Newest
- Oldest
- View Count
- Rating
- Relevance

After making your selections and adding operators be sure to click the Search button in the bottom left corner of the search box instead of the one at the top of the page where you conducted your original search.

Beyond Search

With any luck you will soon have a number of videos that are of interest to you, and YouTube offers ways to keep things manageable and interactive.

All of these management tools require that you be signed in to YouTube. Use the same Google account email and password as with all other Google Tools and web sites.

Once you are signed in you will see your account name in the upper right corner of the screen. Clicking on the drop down menu reveals several management options:

- Account
- My Videos
- Favorites
- Playlists
- Inbox

Start by clicking the Account link which will take you to your "My Account / Account Settings" page. This is where you can manage your account, adjust settings, and customize the YouTube homepage. There are many options available here but we're going to focus on the ones that will get you up and running the quickest.

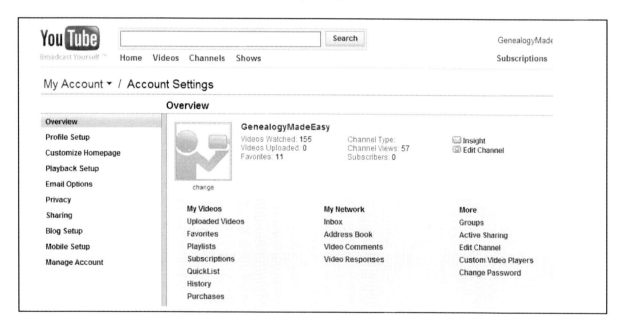

You'll see three major categories in the light blue box in the middle of the screen. To get started, you will want to focus on the first category, which is *My Videos*. The *My Network* category focuses on interacting with other YouTube users, and the *More* category contains more advanced features.

Playlists

Under *My Videos* click *Playlists* - Right now it's empty, so click the "give it a try" link in the center of the page to get started. A playlist is a collection of videos that share common tags. An easy way to begin is to create a playlist for each category of genealogy-themed videos that we discussed at the beginning of this lesson, which I've summarized using appropriate "Playlist Names":

- Historical Events / Vintage Footage
- Family History Documentaries
- Genealogy Instructional Videos
- Archives, Libraries, & Repositories
- Genealogy Experts and Vendors Interviews
- Family History Fun

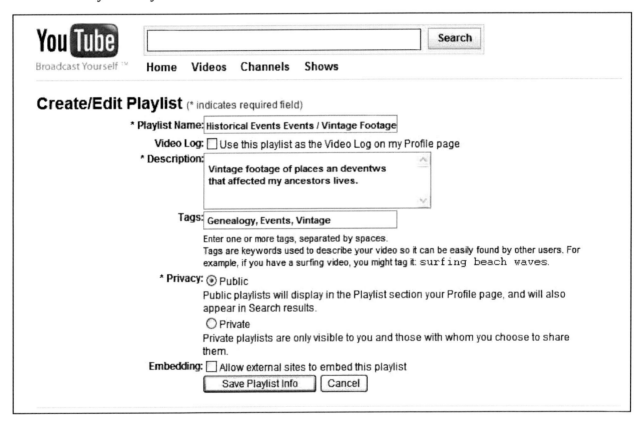

Let's start by creating a Historical Events / Vintage Footage playlist. Type in the Playlist Name as "Historical Events / Vintage Footage." Next type a simple description of the types of videos you plan to add to this playlist. For example:

"Vintage footage of places and events that affected my ancestors lives."

Type a few keywords in the tags field such as Genealogy, Events, and Vintage.

Select the privacy setting you want. If you're unsure how much you want to share with others, click Private, and you can always change your playlist to Public later on. However, making your playlist public could facilitate connecting with other users who are interested in the same videos or topics.

Finally, click the Embedding box if you want other web sites to be able to embed your playlist on their web site. Leave the box unchecked if you do not want to allow that. Click the Save Playlist Info button.

> **QUICK TIP:** If you start to collect a number of videos of events and vintage film footage, consider creating a playlist for each of the surnames you are researching and add the videos to the appropriate family playlist. You can always delete playlists, so play with them until you have playlists that support your research in the best and most organized way.

After clicking the Save button you will now be on the page for the newly created playlist within your account. Here you can manage the videos in your playlist and share them with others if you wish.

Learn more about Playlists
VIDEO: *How to make a playlist – YouTube Help Center*
http://www.youtube.com/watch?v=9DWTF7MJ6H4

Favorites

As you're searching YouTube you will probably come across interesting videos that you like but that don't quite fit into a particular Playlist. Those videos are good candidates to be marked as Favorites.

You'll find the Favorite option under each video. Just click it and a little red heart will appear and you will get a message letting you know that the video has been added to your favorites. To go back to your Favorites in your account just hover your mouse over your user name in the upper right corner of the page and click on Favorites from the drop down menu.

If you decide that you would like to add the newly Favorited video to a playlist, just click the Add to link and select Playlist and a box will pop up where you can select the playlist you want the video to be a part of.

Whenever you want to revisit your Favorite videos or Playlists just hover over your user name and select from the menu, or go to you're My Account and select from the menu on the left.

Below: My Account Example.

Video Sharing

Just like uploading your family tree to a genealogy web site, sharing your family history videos can be a creative way to connect with other researchers across the country that are researching the same family lines.

Your video must meet the following requirements for uploading to YouTube. Your video must be:
- Less than 15 minutes
- Smaller than 2GB in size
- In an acceptable file format (.AVI, .MOV, .WMV and .MPG)

How to upload a video to YouTube:

1. Click the UPLOAD button in the upper right corner of any YouTube page
2. Click the Browse button to browse your computer hard drive for the video file you want to upload (you can upload up to 10 at one time)
3. Click the Upload Video button to start the uploading process
4. As the video is uploading, enter information about your video in the fields provided. The more information you provide, the easier it will be for other users to find and watch your video.
5. Click the Save Changes button to save the updates you've made to the video file

To learn more about uploading your own videos:
VIDEO: *How to Upload a Video to YouTube*
http://www.youtube.com/watch?v=_O7iUiftbKU

A Sample Search

Like with all the other searches we've done so far, the place to start is to determine what it is you want to find. Develop a list of keywords, phrases, and data to draw from as you conduct and refine your search.

For this example I'd like to find some vintage footage of towns in England where the Cooke ancestors lived. First stop will be the seaside town of Margate, Kent where they owned a hotel in the in late 19th and early 20th centuries.

Here's a list of terms that may come in handy as I attempt to find these types of videos:
- Vintage
- Film
- Footage
- Reel

It's also a good idea to take a quick look at a map and make a list of some of the towns and location names adjoining and associated with Margate:
- Ramsgate
- Thanet
- Cliftonville
- Broadstairs
- Kent
- Westgate-on-sea
- Birchington

Here's the first search attempt: ***Margate film footage***

At first glance the results don't look very promising. But upon closer inspection of the nearly 40 results there are a few possibilities worth looking into:
- Margate in the 1950s & 1960s (a little later than I wanted, but worth noting)
- Memories of Dreamland Margate ("rare footage")
- Ramsgate Life on Film_Part 1

A quick click on *Ramsgate Life* (http://www.youtube.com/watch?v=TnoqGlRIPK8) and within the first few moments of the video it says 1920 – 2009. Soon it launches into quite old footage. A look at the Description box gives more information about what I can expect to see in this video:

> *"I have made an all-new film documenting the events of a fantastic place in Thanet. This extraordinary footage shows events from HMS Thanet's arrival in Ramsgate Harbor in 1919, to visits from Royalty and Ramsgate in War time..."*

This sounds like a good match, and a click of the Playlist link beneath the video allows me to add this video to my playlist for later review.

Once you find a video that is of interest to you, there are additional things you can do to capitalize on it to lead you to more videos that fit your criteria. You've heard the saying "there's more where that came from." Well, that is often the case on YouTube.

How to find similar content based on a found video:

1. Related Videos
Check the Related Videos column on the right side of the video page. YouTube automatically groups videos based on how they were tagged. In this case Parts 2 & 3 of "Ramsgate Life" are listed, as well as a video called "Ramsgate Remembered." The screen shots of the videos allow you to quickly scan them for those vintage black and white images we would be interested in.

By scrolling through the Related Videos we also come across a video called *British Pathe Archive* that looks like vintage footage. Pathe was a very early film company and would be a good term to add to our keyword search list since there are likely other videos available from the Pathe Archive.

2. Related Users
There's also a good chance that the user who uploaded this video may have uploaded others that we would find interesting. By clicking the linked user's name JLMdesigns, we are taken to their YouTube channel where we can then browse all of their uploaded videos.

According to the description of the video, this user seems very interested in the Ramsgate area. So once we arrive at their channel, we may also want to view their Favorites lists or other Playlists if available.

The bottom line: *Everything on YouTube is interconnected. Traditional search is only half the search. The other half is following the links for content that interests you to other related content.*

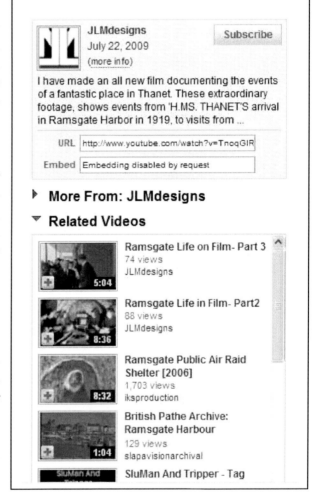

To continue this search for old footage of the Margate area, try different combinations of the keywords and locations, incorporating traditional operators as needed to focus in on the videos you want.

Let's try another search on a different subject and find some videos that will help us prepare for a visit to the Allen County Library in Fort Wayne, Indiana.

Initial Search: Allen County Library
Results: 120
One of the top results is a video called *Genealogy Center, Allen County Public Library* (http://www.youtube.com/watch?v=tcqDqc0SXgo). By clicking on the user's name we find this video was actually uploaded by the Allen County Library and is one of 120 that they have on their YouTube channel. Plenty to explore there!

Revised Search: Allen County Library family history
Results: 6
The top two videos look good:

Tour of Allen County Public Library
        http://www.youtube.com/watch?v=zwPx61I4eVg

This Week in America, Curt Witcher part 2
        http://www.youtube.com/watch?v=OkBegNVby-4

By clicking on each of these videos and exploring the listed related videos and the user channels we can find our way to more and more relevant videos, many of which we may want to add to our *Archives, Libraries, & Repositories* playlist.

> **QUICK TIP:** Do a search for the word "cemetery" and you will find almost 25,000 videos! Better yet, type in the name of the cemetery where your ancestors are buried. You might just be surprised at what you find! Then try the same for the churches they attended.

Keys to Success

- **Follow related links.** When you find a video you like, follow the associated links to explore additional related content.

- **Make use of your free account.** Create playlists to organize your videos and research. Mark your favorite videos, particularly if they are about a town, cemetery, family, or other research topic that you are interested in. Remember: when other users follow links that interest them they may very well end up on your playlist or channel. When they find videos you've marked as favorites they will know you are interested in that family or topic as well and may leave a comment that could lead to a research connection.

- **Keep an open mind.** The number of genealogical topics that might appear in a YouTube video is only limited by your imagination.

- **Check back from time to time.** Use the "Uploaded" drop down menu on the Advanced Search page to check for the newest uploads for your searches.

CHAPTER 13
Google Earth Overview

Google describes the Google Earth tool this way: "Google Earth lets you fly anywhere on Earth to view satellite imagery, maps, terrain, 3D buildings, from galaxies in outer space to the canyons of the ocean. You can explore rich geographical content, save your toured places, and share with others."

From a genealogist's perspective, however, Google Earth offers so much more than virtually flying to locations around the world. It has the power to document your ancestors' lives in a multi-media fashion. And it lends itself very well to collaboration with other researchers and sharing your family history with your loved ones. In this chapter we will explore Google Earth as a 360-degree, 3-dimensional way to view your ancestor's world.

Google Earth is different from the other Google tools because it is actual software that you install on your computer. However, like all Google tools, the standard version of Google Earth is absolutely free (and that's very uncommon for high powered geographic software).

Google Earth Pro is the advanced version geared for business use and currently runs $400. For more information go to: http://www.google.com/enterprise/earthmaps/earth_pro.html. For genealogy, we'll have everything we need in the free version.

How to Download and Install Google Earth

1. Go to http://earth.google.com/
2. Click the blue Download Google Earth button

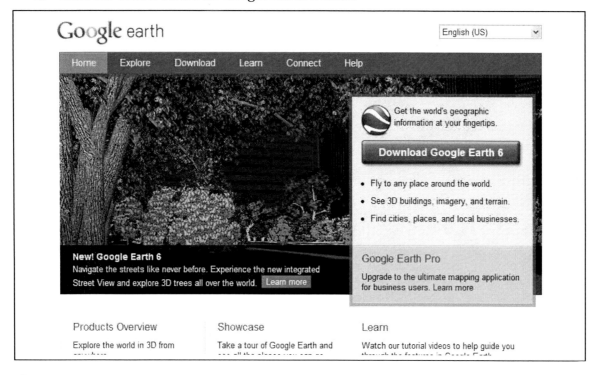

From the Install Google Earth with Google Updater page:
3. Unclick the Include Google Chrome box if you don't wish to install the Google Chrome browser
4. Read the Terms and Conditions
5. If you agree to them, click the Agree and Download button
6. Follow the installation guide
7. When complete click the Run Google Earth button

(Note: The installer automatically installed a Google Earth icon on your desktop. Just click it to launch the program in the future.)

Each time you open Google Earth the Tip box will appear and provide tips for using the program. These can help you get up to speed quickly. If you want to scroll through a number of tips just click the Prev Tip and Next Tip buttons in the bottom left corner. If you don't wish to have the Tip box appear at the start just uncheck the *Show tips at startup* box.

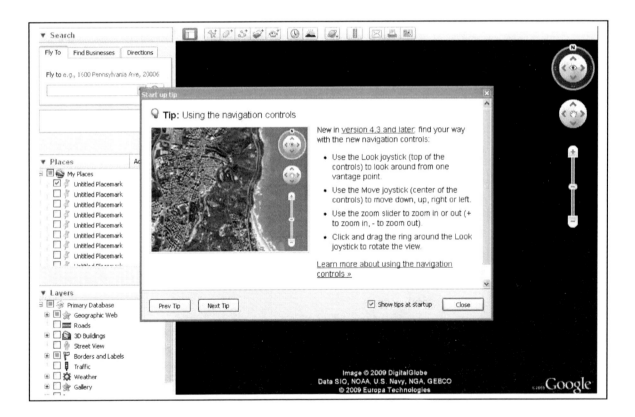

Before you get started using Google earth, return to your Internet browser, which should be opened to Google Earth's *Thank You* page. This page appears after software installation. There are some good resources here to take note of:

- A tour of 3D buildings in the Google Earth Gallery
- The Google Earth Sightseer Newsletter

- Earth Plug-in for your Internet browser

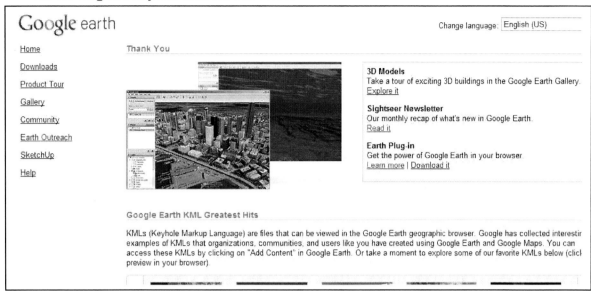

And finally if you cross down to the bottom of the Thank You page you'll find links to some recommended Google Earth blogs with additional tips and ideas.

The Software – Panels

The Google Earth viewing area is broken up into panels. Along the left side of your screen you'll find three panels:

- Search
- Places
- Layers

Across the top of the main screen called the "3D Viewer" is a tool bar with additional features operated by toggle buttons. By hovering your mouse over a tool bar button you will see the label telling you its function. They are:

- Hide side panels
- Add Placemark
- Add Polygon
- Add Path
- Add Image Overlay
- Record A Tour
- Show Historical Imagery

- Show sunlight across landscape
- Switch between Earth, Sky and Planets
- Show Ruler
- Email
- Print
- View in Google Map

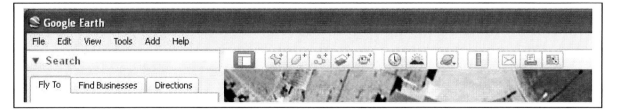

While working in Google Earth you will probably want to keep these panels visible. However they can be closed to create a larger viewing area.

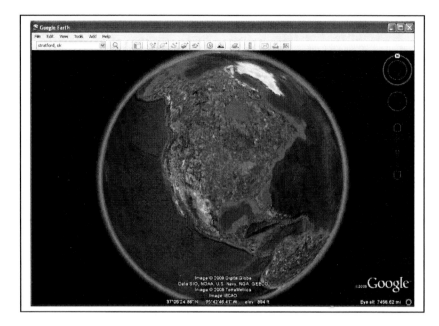

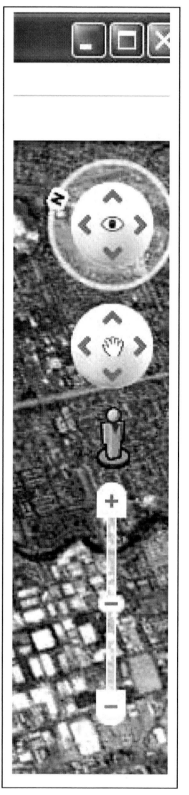

In the upper right corner of the 3D Viewer you will find the Navigation Controls.

These let you zoom, loom, and move around. Google Earth does not require north be at the top. Click and drag the ring around the top button to rotate our view. The "N" ring around the top Navigation button controls direction. Whenever you want to return north to the top of the viewer simply click the north-up button to reset the view.

The center of the top button looks like an eye, and is referred to as the Look joystick. Use it to look around from a single vantage point, just like if you were turning your head. After clicking an arrow on the Look joystick, move the mouse around on the joystick to change the direction of motion.

The middle button is the Move joystick, which allows you to move your position on the Earth from one place to another. Click an arrow on Move to look in that direction and then move the mouse around on the joystick to change the direction of motion.

On the bottom of the Navigation Controls you will find the zoom slider. This allows you to zoom in and out by moving the slider handle or by clicking the plus and minus signs. As you move closer to the ground, Google Earth tilts to change your viewing angle to be parallel to the Earth's surface.

The arrow button on your keyboard also allows you to navigate in Google Earth. Best of all you can just click with your mouse. Two clicks zooms in, and two right-clicks zooms out. To stop the zoom, just click once on the viewer.

Learn more about navigating in Google Earth
VIDEO: *Navigating in Google Earth*
http://www.youtube.com/watch?v=rd2uXE1fTI0

Search Panel

To locate a geographic location, just type the location in the "Fly To" search box. This could be a town and state, a zip code, or other place name. If Google Earth finds multiple possible matches it will list them in the box below so that you can select the one you want. The places you search will remain listed in the box, available to be returned to with a simple click. To clear the searches from the box, click the X in the bottom right corner of the box in the Search panel.

Also in the Search panel you will find two additional types of searches:

- *Find Businesses* – great for finding local area businesses
- *Directions* – By typing your *From* location and a *To* location and clicking the search button (the magnifying glass) Google Earth will instantly map out the journey turn by turn

Places Panel

This is where you locate, save, organize, and revisit your placemarks and files. The Add Content button in the right corner of this panel allows you to import content from the online KML Gallery, containing community-created content files that you can view using Google Earth or Google Maps. You can also create and submit your own KML files to the gallery.

Learn more about KML at http://google.earth.com/kml
Learn more about KML Gallery at
http://www.google.com/gadgets/directory?synd=earth&cat=featured&preview=on

Layers Panel and Points of Interest

Google Earth can complete a wide range of tasks. In this book we are going to focus on features that support executing and reporting our genealogy research. However, Layers are a key feature of Google Earth and deserve a quick review.

Layers provide a collection of points of geographic interest that can be displayed over your viewing area. You'll find the Layers feature in the Layers panel on the bottom left side of your screen. Layers content is created by Google or its content partners.

To display all points of interest (or POIs) within a layer click the box next to the Layer title. POIs within the layer can be selected and unselected the same way. To open a Layer category just click the plus sign next to the label to open the layer folder, and the minus sign to close the layer folder.

You will likely want to experiment at some point with all of the available layers, but for now here are some genealogically helpful ones to give particular notice.

Geographic Web

- Wikipedia
- Places
- Roads

Borders and Labels

- Borders (great for viewing county lines)
- Alternative Place Names

Gallery

- Gigapan Photos
- Gigapxl Photos
- Google Book Search
- (indicating books related to that geographic area)

Rumsey Historical Maps

- About the Maps
- Map Finder (allows you to lay an available map over a geographic area to see it as it once was)

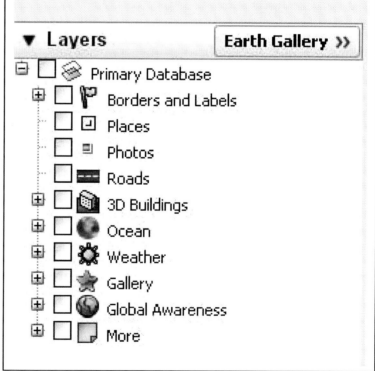

Travel and Tourism

- Webcams.travel (allows you to view live shots where available)

Places of Interest

- Geographic Features
- Schools
- Places of Worship (within this category you will find Cemeteries)

(Note: Many of these POIs could be of interest if you are planning a visit)

Terrain

> **QUICK TIP:** Each Layer has different requirements on how close you must be zoomed in on a geographic area to be able to view the POIs. For instance, if you're trying to view buildings you will have to be zoomed in close enough for buildings to be seen. If you're having difficulty viewing layers and POIs, zoom in and out until you find what you're looking for.

Finding Ancestral Homes and Locations

When you're working with the census you can often extract the address of the home where your ancestor lived. Google Earth offers you a powerful way to get an up close and personal view of that location. Here's an example:

According to the 1910 U.S. Federal Population Census, my great grandparents lived at 288 Connecticut St., San Francisco, CA.

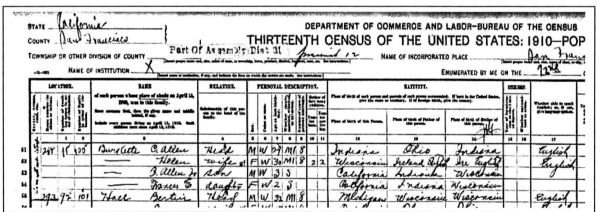

By typing the complete address in the Fly To box in the Search Panel and clicking the search button, Google Earth will zoom in to that exact location on the map. Using the navigation controls you can zoom in even further.

By clicking the Push Pin icon in the Tool Bar you can mark the exact location on the map, label the pin, and type in a complete description.

Each time you click on the pin all of that data will appear in a box.

You will find the saved pushpin file in the Places panel.

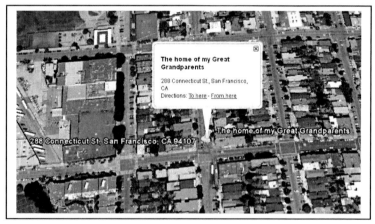

Historical Imagery & Map Overlays

Historical Imagery

A new feature in Google Earth is Historical Imagery. Click the clock icon on the Tool Bar and a slider bar will appear at the top of the map indicating how far back map images are available for your location. In the case of San Francisco we can turn the hands of time back to 1946 image. To return to modern day just unclick the clock icon or move the slider back up to the current year. Unfortunately there are a very limited number of historical satellite images available.

Historical Maps

You can go even further back in time with the Rumsey Historical Maps Overlay, which you will find in the Layers Panel.

Working with the address 288 Connecticut St., zoom back out to view the entire city of San Francisco. Select the Rumsey Historical Maps box in the Layers Panel. Navigation icons will appear on the map if historical maps are available for your location. If you don't see any at first try zooming further out so you can see more of the area.

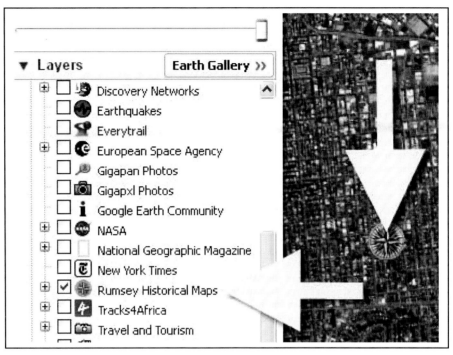

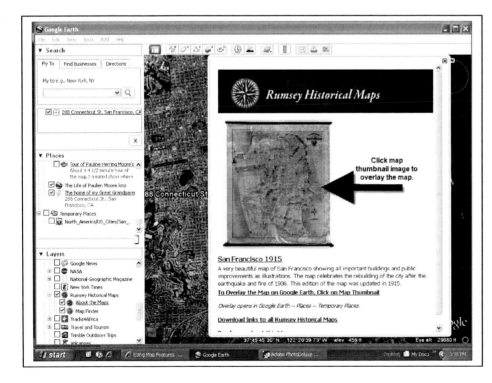

Hovering over the icon reveals the date of the available map. In this case there is a 1915 San Francisco Map overlay available. Click on the icon and a pop up window will appear with an image and details about the map.

To overlay the map on Google Earth, simply click on the map thumbnail image.

The map will spread out across the area lining up as closely as possible with the current day map. The map will resize as you zoom in and out, always maintaining proper proportions. *(image below)*

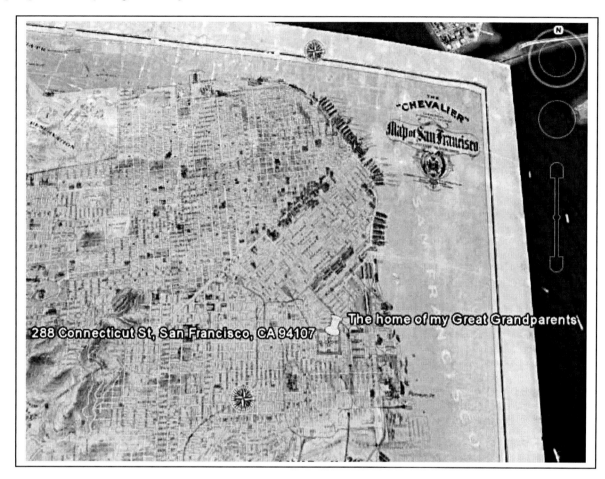

By zooming in again we can tour the Connecticut Street neighborhood where they lived around the time they lived there.

How to Save the Placemark and Historic Map in the Places Panel:

1. Click on My Places to select it
2. Right click on My Places and select ADD – FOLDER
3. A New Folder window will pop up where you can name your folder and enter a detailed description of its contents. (You may want to have a folder for each surname you research)
4. Click OK
5. Scroll down the Places Panel and you will see your new folder under My Places
6. Click the location marked with the placemark push pin and drag and drop

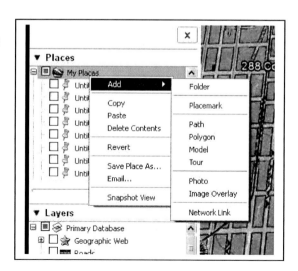

it into the new folder

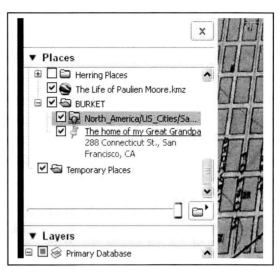

7. The box for the place is currently checked. Click it to uncheck and the placemark will be removed from the map. The box operates as a toggle switch for that location.
8. Scroll down further to the Temporary Places folder in the Places Panel
9. Locate the Historical Map overlay that was applied
10. Click, drag, and drop it into your folder. The overlay can be removed and applied again by clicking and unclicking its checkbox.
11. Select *Save Place As* from the menu
12. Name the place and save it to the desired location on your hard drive

Photos

If you happen to have an old family photo of a place (e.g. the family homestead or business) then Google Earth has something very unique to offer. Photos can be added to maps in 3D.

How to Add a Photo to a Placemark:

The simplest way to add photos to your maps is to host your photos on a photo sharing website that automatically generates the html code you will need. For this example we are using http://www.Photobucket.com.

1. Upload your photo to Photobucket
2. Hover your mouse over the image to review the drop down box
3. Click the HTML code field and the code will automatically be copied
4. Open your map in Google Earth
5. Right click the icon that you want to associate the photograph with to open the Edit Placemark box
6. Paste the HTML code into the Description field
7. Add additional text or story if desired
8. Click OK
9. Click on the icon and the image and text will appear in a viewing box

See It In Action!
VIDEO: *Add a Photo to Google Earth*
http://www.youtube.com/watch?v=gki8VGrMxTw
VIDEO: *Add Photos and Image Overlays* By Earth Outreach
http://www.youtube.com/watch?v=D9LcwbwQgzk

The Power of Street View

A real life application is the best way to convey the power of the street view feature in Google Earth. Here's an example of how I used street view to find my Great Grandparents home and store 100 years later and identify a vintage photograph at the same time.

I have had this photo of my great grandfather holding my grandfather in late 1906 in San Francisco for over thirty years but have never been sure where it was taken. Because the 1910 census is the closest U.S. Population Schedule available, I went back to it and extracted the address that the census taker wrote in the left hand margin: 288 Connecticut St., San Francisco, CA.

The first step in Google earth is to go to the Search Panel and Fly to the address. It's important to zoom in close enough to see the street and be able to distinguish building outlines.

As you zoom closer, the Street View "person" icon will appears in the upper right corner of the 3D Viewer above the zoom tool. The Street View icon debuted with Google Earth Version 6.0. (Prior to that Street View was activated in the Layers Panel.) Click on the icon and drag and drop it on map. As you drag it over the map, dark blue lines will appear in locations across the map that have Street View available.

I zoomed in on the address and used the navigation tools to try to get the same perspective as my original photo. That way I could compare the two side by side to see if it was a match. (A front-on view of the building would not have been helpful in the case of my photo as you can see.)

(Image Below: Drag and Drop the Street View "Man" icon onto the map. Dark lines appear on the streets indicating that Street View is available. Note that some trees already look 3D.)

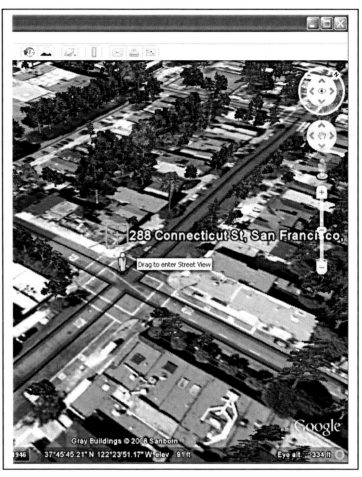

Visualize yourself standing on the location. By clicking and grabbing the image you can spin around in a complete circle and see everything from that position just as if you were standing there yourself! Notice that Google Earth displays the address where you are "standing." At the bottom of the screen you'll see which direction you are looking (North, South, East, West.) Grab the image and turn the view to look straight down the road and the name of the street appears in the center of the road. This is very helpful because it is easy to get a bit disoriented. Look for these cues from Google Earth to keep track of where you are.

To view the street from another position, just double click on that spot on the screen and you will be "transported" there visually with a full 360-degree view. The address of the viewing location will always appear in the upper right corner of the viewer.

There are other ways to navigate in addition to grabbing and dragging the image. Use the Right and Left arrows on your keyboard to turn right and left. Use the Up arrow to zoom in and the Down arrow to zoom out. You can exit Street View anytime by clicking the Exit Street View button in the very top right corner of the screen.

Finding the Location

Regular map view indicates the address location on the map, but Street View does not mark each building in the image with an address. Therefore, it can be challenging to identify where the exact address location is in the 360-degree Street View. You may need to jump back and forth between Street View and the regular map view to compare landmarks. Locate the address on the regular map. Is there an empty lot next door? A large tree in front? Use the ring around the top "North" navigation button to tilt your view for more comparison.

Since my case was in San Francisco, I had the added advantage of the hills to help me determine where to look first. You'll notice in my original photo that the road slopes downward in to the distance. That eliminates two of the four streets I could see from Street View since they both sloped uphill. Of the two remaining streets one sloped far more than the street in the photo, so I decided to examine the other street first.

Using the photo as my guide I looked down the left side of the street, keeping an eye out for any distinguishing building elements. It didn't take long to notice a tall building with a similar roof overhang to the one in the photo. Soon I was able to match up several points on each of the images.

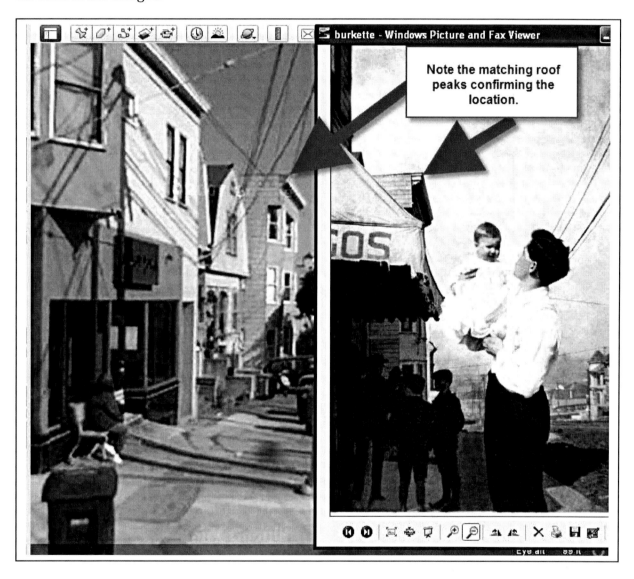

My great grandparents moved several times in the first decade of the 20th century. Google Earth provides the quickest way for visiting the various locations, comparing images, and determining the exact location. Photographs can be come a little less mysterious with Google Earth.

Ground-Level View

Also new in Google Earth 6.0 is Ground-Level view. After you activate Street View by clicking, dragging and dropping the Street View icon onto the map, a mini toolbar will appear in the upper right corner of the 3D Viewer. You can toggle between the person icon (Street View) and the new building icon (Ground-Level View.) You can also go back to the regular map by clicking the Exit Street View button.

Ground-Level View provides a new way to see all the 3D data that Google and the large number of individuals around the world using Google Sketch-Up to create 3D models have added to Google Earth. To get the most out of Ground-Level View, click the box next to 3D Buildings in the Layers panel to activate them.

Try it for yourself:
In addition to large cities like San Francisco that feature large numbers of 3D building in Google Earth, Walt Disney World in Orlando, Florida is a great place to try out the features of Ground-Level View. Type Epcot Center in the Fly To box and press Enter. After Google Earth zooms in on Epcot, drag and drop the Street View icon on to the spot on the screen where you want to begin using Street View and Ground-Level View.

The first thing you will notice is that the buildings and many of the trees are now 3D. You can navigate quickly and easily by using your keyboard:

Use the Arrow Keys to drive around
- Page Up Key and Page Down Keys will drive you faster
- Holding the ALT key down along with the Arrow Keys will move you more slowly
- Holding the CTRL (or Command key in Mac) down along with the Up/Down Arrows will tilt your view

Your mouse can also be used to navigate:
- Use the Scroll Wheel on your mouse to "drive"
- Click / Drag the screen to move around and change directions.
- Double-Click on any location in front of you to fly directly there.

Epcot is also unique in that you can actually go inside some buildings (though the contents are incomplete) and by clicking on each feature (rides, hotels, etc.) you will usually get a pop-up window providing you with more information, and even videos!

The Future

We can expect to see Ground-Level View expand across the globe and cities, communities and even historic locations create rich content to Google Earth. This is only the beginning!

CHAPTER 14
Google Earth – Ancestral Homes & Locations

Geography and genealogy go hand in hand. It's impossible to locate records or follow family lines without understanding land formations, boundaries, jurisdictions and distances. Decisions that directly affected your family for generations consistently revolve around geography such as:

- Where records are created and stored
- The path chosen for migration
- Locations selected for settlement
- Division of farms and property in probate

Because land itself doesn't move, it's one of the few elements of our ancestors' lives that we can always count on. Consider an old photograph. Buildings may have changed but the surrounding landmarks such as hills, valleys and rock formations still stand today and can aid in identification.

Finding Ancestral Homes and Locations

For most researchers it just isn't financially feasible to personally travel to all of the locations where your ancestors lived. The good news is that Google Earth can provide you with a "virtual reality" type experience that is as close to being there as your computer can take you.

Plot an Ancestor's Home

Let's start with an address that you probably have and very likely are familiar with – the house where one of your grandparents lived. If by chance you don't have that address, conduct this exercise for one of your childhood homes.

1. In the Search panel type the address in the Fly To box and click the magnifying glass icon

2. The globe in the 3D viewer will start to turn and very quickly will zoom in to that location

3. Put a placemark on that location so you keep track of the exact spot by clicking the Placemark button in the Viewer Toolbar

4. When the New Placemark box opens, label the placemark with the exact street address and your Grandparents' names

5. Click OK.

You have now located your first ancestral home on Google Earth. But this is only the beginning...

Getting a Closer Look

While it is certainly interesting to locate an ancestor's home on the globe, it's difficult to see much detail from the virtual sky looking down over the area. To get an up close and personal look at a location we will need to employ Google Earth's Street View function.

Street View offers you a panoramic view from various positions on the street. Launched in May of 2007 by Google.com, Street View first featured a few major cities in the U.S.

Today nearly every street in America is represented in Street View, and it is quickly spreading around the world.

Just how does Google do it? They have developed a fleet of specially adapted cars with nine directional cameras attached to the tops at a height of about 2.5 meters. These cars drive up and down each street snapping photographs from all directions every few seconds. When faced with narrow streets such as in Rome in Italy, Google Trikes (tricycles) were similarly equipped to make the journey. They've even employed snowmobiles where necessary in cold climate areas!

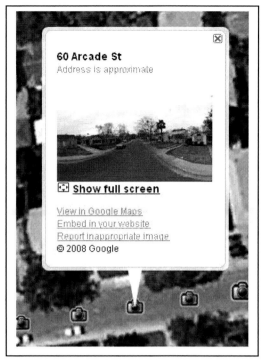

View Your Ancestor's Home With Street View
(This example utilizes Google Earth Versions Prior to 6.0. See previous chapter for using 6.0 Street View)

Start at your ancestor's home that you identified in the previous exercise.

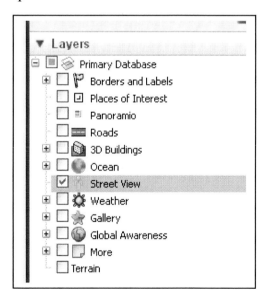

1. Go to the Layers Panel and select Street View from the list of options

2. Zoom in closer to the location until camera icons appear on the street. Zoom in close enough to see the cameras directly in front of the home.

3. Hover your mouse over the camera icon directly in front of the house. This will reveal the approximate address where the street view photos were taken.

4. Click the camera icon once to reveal the pop up dialogue box. The box includes:
   a. A photo of the location
   b. The approximate address
   c. A link that shows the image's full screen street view
   d. A link to plot the location in Google Maps
   e. A link to get the code to embed the image on your website
   f. The date the image was taken and copyrighted.

5. Click the Show Full Screen link to enter street view (you can also go directly to street view by double clicking a camera icon.)

6. You will notice that it takes a moment to process. Soon the image appears as a sphere representing the panoramic nature of the view you are about to get. Then Google Earth appears to zoom directly inside the sphere.

When the image completes the process, visualize yourself standing inside the spherical photo at the specific point on that street. You can turn around 360-degrees standing in that one position and see from any vantage point within that spherical photo. You are now "virtually visiting" that neighborhood!

There are two key ways to maneuver your way around Street View.

1. Simply grab the screen with your mouse and drag it the direction you want to look

2. Hover your mouse in the upper right corner of the image (near the zoom tool) and a Photo Viewer Controller will appear. Grab the white outlined box and drag it around within the Photo Viewer Controller to move the entire image easily.

See It For Yourself:
VIDEO: *Street View in Google Earth*
http://www.youtube.com/watch?v=_WN
xe75rkUA&feature=player_embedded#

It can be a little confusing getting your
directional bearings once you are in
Street View. Look for house numbers on the house as well as the curb. To get a closer look
at a particular area double click on the spot on the image and Google Earth will slowly
zoom in closer.

You can also hover your mouse on the camera icons, which still appear down each street
to get the approximate street address. You can get the address for the Street View
spherical photo you are currently viewing from in the upper right corner of the image.

QUICK TIP: In general, even-numbered addresses
will be on one side, and odd-numbered addresses
on the opposite side of the street. If the house you
are looking for doesn't have a street number on
the house or curb, look to the houses on either
side to deduce the correct home.

Exploring Additional Locations

Now that we've located an ancestor's home and explored it up close with Street View, it's
time to start pondering other types of family history locations that might be worthy of a
virtual visit.

Here are some initial ideas for ancestral locations to explore:

- Homes
- Villages
- Farms
- Homesteads
- Businesses
- Photograph Locations
- Places of Worship

...and the list goes on.

As a genealogist, you probably have a lot more of these locations at your fingertips than you realize.

Places to look:

- Your genealogy database. Chances are over time you have entered addresses based on the records you've located.
- Original Records
- Google Search

Practice Makes Perfect

Select one grandparent and spend some time plotting out locations that were pertinent throughout his or her life. Mark each location with a Placemark pushpin. In the next chapter we will put a plan in place for saving, organizing and sharing those locations, as well as the other places we find. It will be the foundation for your Google Earth treasury of family history geography.

CHAPTER 15
Google Earth – Saving, Organizing, & Sharing

Now that you've explored some ancestral locations in Google Earth it's a good time to stop and think about organization. As you progress through these chapters you will soon begin to collect locations and information that you will want to keep and easily retrieve. Laying a solid organizational foundation for your work in Google Earth now will pay off big dividends down the road.

Placemarks - Creating, Naming, and Organizing

You may have noticed in the previous chapter that each time you added a Placemark pushpin to the globe it was added to the My Places folder in the Places panel. Look for the yellow pushpin icons in the Places panel. You will notice that if you labeled the placemark when the New Placemark dialogue box popped up, the name you entered appears as the name of the pushpin in the Places panel. If you skipped that step, the pushpin will simply be named Untitled Placemark.

How to Create and Name a Placemark:

1. Fly to the location of your choice on the map
2. Click the Add Placemark button on the 3D Viewer toolbar
3. Do not enter a name
4. Click OK
5. Look to the Places panel and locate the Placemark you just created
6. Right click on the Placemark in the Place Panel
7. Select Rename
8. Type in the name
9. Press the Enter key on your keyboard

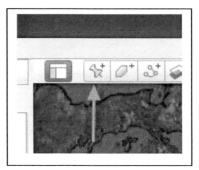

Now you have the flexibility to name and rename your Placemarks as needed to keep them descriptive and organized.

Folders

It doesn't take long after adding a few Placemarks to Google Earth to determine that some organization will be needed. There is a simple way to avoid piling up all your locations in the My Places folder. Creating sub-folders will help you store and organize your

Placemarks. Folder management is very much like the folder management you do on your computer's hard drive, except you can do it within Google Earth.

See It For Yourself!
Video: *Organize Your Hard Drive Video*
At the Family Tree Magazine You Tube Channel
Learn the basic concepts of organizing digital family history files on your computer hard drive.

Watch the video at:
http://www.youtube.com/watch?v=oWF
DITBusPM

In the case of filing files in Google Earth, I recommend creating surname file folders. Start with the surnames you search the most. Add folders as needed. There is no limit to how many you can have!

How to Create Surname Folders:

1. Click on My Places in the Places Panel to highlight that folder
2. Right Click to reveal menu options
3. Select Add – New Folder
4. The New Folder box will pop up
5. Name the folder. (i.e. SMITH, JONES, etc. Focus on the surnames you intend to search first.)
6. In the Description area type in information that will assist you in understanding the family line this folder refers to
   a. (ex: the Smith family of Ohio, with origins in Germany. Year of immigration: 1860. Earliest head of household in database is John Smith – person #461.)
7. Check two check boxes allowing greater visibility in the Places Panel:
   a. Allow this folder to be expanded
   b. Show contents as options.
      (These can always be removed at a later time.)
8. Click OK

QUICK TIP: If you anticipate using Google Earth for other activities in addition to Genealogy, create a Genealogy folder first and then take the previous steps to create folders within the Genealogy folder.

You now have your first surname folder in your Places Panel. Go ahead and take a few moments to create a few more just to get comfortable with the process for making folders.

When you identify a location that you want to mark and save, click on the folder in the Places Panel where you want to save that Placemark before creating it. By selecting the folder first, the new Placemark will be saved to that surname folder.

How to Move Placemarks Between Folders:

If by chance you end up with a placemark in the wrong folder it can easily be moved:

1. Click on the Placemark in the Places Panel
2. Drag it to the appropriate folder
3. Drop it into the folder

Similarly, folders can also be dragged and dropped into other folders.

How to Delete Files or Folders:

Files and folders within the Places Panel can be as easily deleted as they are created. To delete a file or an entire folder:

1. Right click on the file or folder
2. Select Delete from the menu
3. Click OK in the pop up box

Organizing Files

Just as there are a variety of record types in our genealogical research that must be filed in folders on our hard drive, so are there a variety of media files that can be generated within Google Earth that should be filed and organized.

A recommended method for incorporating these items is modeled after basic hard drive organization as previously described (and illustrated in the recommended video.) By creating a folder for each media type within each Surname folder, you will have a place to safely store your work, and easily retrieve it in the future.

Saving Images

It is inevitable that as you begin to create and save your maps you will want to share them with your friends, family, and other researchers that you may be collaborating with. Or perhaps you would like to include them in a family history book, chart, blog or family website, slideshow, or video. There are endless possibilities of how to incorporate Google Earth maps into your family history storytelling!

The good news is that jpeg images can be saved directly from Google earth for just such applications.

How to Save an Image:

1. In the Places panel, activate the image by clicking the box next to it.
2. Zoom in until you get the perspective of the location that you desire
3. In the Layers Panel, activate Street View by checking the box next to it
4. Activate Street View by clicking on and dragging the Street View person icon and dropping it on the area
5. Position the view as desired
6. Click the Hide Sidebar button in the 3D Viewer Toolbar so that you will have the map image only
7. From the menu select File
8. Click Image
9. Click Save Image
10. In the Save As box navigate to the place on your hard drive where you want to save the image
11. Type a name in the File Name field
12. Click OK

View your image by locating it on your hard drive and double clicking on it.

Image Below: JPEG image taken from Street View

Because this is a JPEG picture file you can use it anywhere you would normally include a JPEG file (i.e. websites, PowerPoint presentations, blogs, etc.). And of course if you want to edit the image you can open it in any photo-editing program and edit it before you use it.

Copying Images

Sometimes you will only need a copy of an image to quickly paste into another program, such as a PowerPoint presentation. In that type of situation you don't necessarily need to save it to your hard drive, which takes up storage space.

How to Copy an Image from Google Earth:

1. From the Google Earth menu click Edit
2. Click Copy Image (this copies the image to your computer's clipboard temporarily)
3. Open the program that you want to add the image to (ex: PowerPoint)
4. Paste the image (Control + V on your keyboard)

You can use this technique for any program on your computer that allows the Copy and Paste function.

Emailing Locations

Sharing images via email has become second nature for most of us. However, when it comes to emailing maps directly from Google Earth there is some good news and some bad news. The good news is that you can email images. The bad news is that (as of this writing) the Email button on the Google Earth toolbar doesn't always work properly.

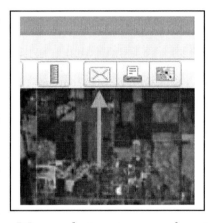

Mac users have noted that the Email function usually works. But sometimes PC users report a different story. Occasionally an error message saying Google Earth couldn't email the image pops up. If you are a Mac user, or a PC user fortunate enough not to encounter the error message, all you have to do is click the email button in the toolbar at the top of the screen and Google Earth automatically attaches the image that currently appears on the screen to an email message.

Both image files (i.e. JPEG) and View / Placemark Files (i.e. KMZ) can be emailed. KMZ files are specific to viewing in Google Earth. If you want to email a Placemark you can also right-click on the placemark and select Email from the list. The recipient will receive an email with a KMZ file attached that opens in Google Earth.

If you do run into trouble with emailing images, there is a work around:

1. Save the image to your computer (as described on the previous page)
2. Open your preferred email program

3. Attach the image from your hard drive to the email
4. Click Send

It's a few extra steps but still gets the job done.

Printing

Printing capabilities are also limited within Google Earth. While you can print what appears in the 3D Viewer (i.e. anything that appears on the globe,) printing from Street View is not available. Again, the work around to this would be to save the image first to your computer's hard drive and print from a photo-editing program.

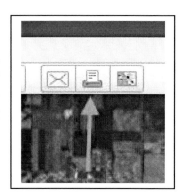

The Print feature can be found in two places:
- The Print button on the toolbar
- In the menu under File – Print

Keys to Success

As you can see Google Earth offers some easy methods to share your geographical family history in new and exciting ways. Take the time before going on to the next chapter to commit to your file organizational strategy, and create the folders you will need to execute it. Then as we continue on in the lessons, stay committed to keeping your files and folders uniformly labeled and filed.

Now that you are familiar with the methods for saving and sharing your image files you are ready to move into the next chapter where we really start to unleash the genealogical power of Google Earth. There will be many things to be shared with family and researchers alike!

Quick Tip – Font Sizing

If you find the small lettering of the labels on Google Earth a challenge to read, here's a quick solution:

1. From the menu click Tools
2. Click Options
3. Select the 3D View Tab
4. In the Labels/Icon Size box select Large
5. Click Apply
6. Click OK

Image Below: Changing the Font Size in Google Earth

www.GenealogyGems.com

CHAPTER 16
Google Earth – Historic Images & Maps

On the surface Google Earth appears to be a modern day virtual view of our world. But there's more as you dig deeper. Geographic history is an important element of the program, and it's available in a couple of different forms: Historical Imagery and Rumsey Historical Maps.

Historical Imagery

Historical Imagery was first introduced in version 5.0 of Google Earth. It allows users to go back in time and study earlier stages of a location. You can view your ancestor's neighborhoods, home towns, and other relevant places and see how they've changed over time.

Image Below: The Historical Imagery Button on the 3D Viewer Toolbar

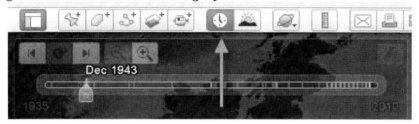

Historical Imagery includes items such as aerial and satellite photographs from government fly-overs and other sources. But, one of the limitations of the Historical Imagery feature is that it can only go back as far as satellite images are available. If you are fortunate enough to find that Historical Imagery is available for the location you are researching, it can be very illuminating. By using the Historical Imagery slider function, you can now travel back through time to see how a place looked decades ago. For example, images taken in 1943 show the effect of wartime bombing on more than 35 European towns and cities, and are available through Google Earth's Historical Imagery.

How to Access Historical Imagery:

Let's look at an example of a European city damaged during WWII.

1. Type Stuttgart, Germany in the Fly To Box in the Search panel

2. Click the Begin Search button

3. Google Earth will zoom in fairly close to the Stuttgart location on the globe

4. Zoom out to get a broader view of the area

5. Click the Show Historical Imagery button on the toolbar (the clock icon), which will activate the slide tool which will appear directly under the toolbar

6. The date on the far right of the slider is very close to today's date. The date on the far left end of the slider is December 1943. Notice the marks on the slider denoting historical images available at various dates between 1943 and today.

7. Click on the slider lever and drag it all the way to the left (Dec. 1943)

8. Notice that the image has changed dramatically. During WWII the city of Stuttgart was subject to over 50 air raids.

9. Zoom out to get a view of Europe. Notice the small squares of gray that appear on the map. These are areas that have historical imagery from 1943.

10. Go to the Layers panel and click the box next to Borders and Labels. This will help you identify the various countries.

11. Zoom in and out to explore the various historical images

12. To return to modern day just unclick the clock icon or move the slider back to the current year

Imagery from 1935 and 1945 for Warsaw in Poland is particularly compelling. The city was amongst those most badly damaged in the war and comparisons with today are striking.

See it for yourself!
Watch a brief video that demonstrates Historical Imagery
VIDEO: *Google Earth 5 – Historical Imagery*
http://www.youtube.com/watch?v=Nv_ScZYnsyw&feature=player_embedded

Rumsey Historical Maps

You can go even further back in time with Rumsey Historical Maps.

http://www.davidrumsey.com/

Google Earth can display maps from the David Rumsey collection in 3D, overlaid on the earth. Each map has been geo-referenced, allowing the old maps to appear in their correct positions on the modern globe. David Rumsey has selected over 200 historical maps in Google Earth Rumsey Historical Maps layer from his collection of more than 150,000 historical maps. In addition, a few maps from collections with which he collaborates have also been added. They range in date from 1680 to  1892 and include 16 historical maps representative of various regions around the world, including Cassini's Globe of 1790, a map of Africa from 1787, and a 1710 Japanese-Chinese map of Asia.

Let's try a simple exercise to see what's available. Keep in mind that all of the features available in the Gallery are available to use while you have an historic map overlay activated. This means that a quick way to locate the items mentioned in the exercise is still to use the Fly To box in the Search Panel. Google Earth will fly you to that location regardless of whether a map overlay has been applied and regardless of whether or not that landmark actually appears on the historic map.

Try It For Yourself: The Streets of San Francisco

1. Type San Francisco in the Fly To box in the Search Panel
2. Zoom back out so that you can see the entire Bay Area
3. In the Layers Panel open the Gallery

4. Select the Rumsey Historical Maps box
5. Navigation icons will appear on the map if historical maps are available for your location. You will see three icons appear in San Francisco.
6. Hover your mouse over each of the three icons to reveal the date of each map
7. Click on the icon for the 1915 San Francisco map
8. A pop up window will appear with an image and details about the map
9. To overlay the map on Google Earth, click on the map thumbnail image

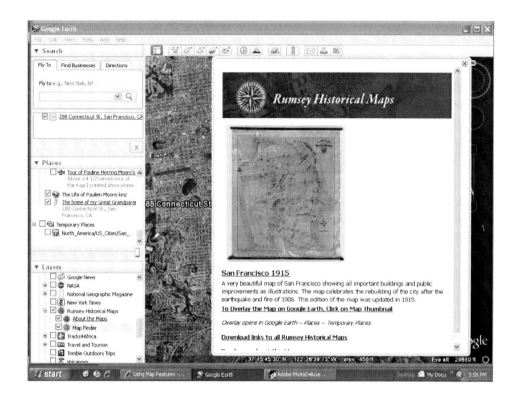

10. The map will spread across the area matching exactly (or as close as possible for older maps that were somewhat inaccurate)
11. Zoom in and out and navigate around the city. Locate the following:
    a. Balboa Park
    b. Golden Gate Park
    c. Union Square
12. Go over to the Places panel and slide the lever at the bottom of the panel all the way to the left. This is a transparency tool and allows you to adjust the transparency back and forth so that you can make comparisons between the historic and modern day maps.

Save the 1915 San Francisco Map to the Places Panel:

13. In the Places panel, click My Places, to select it
14. Right click on My Places and select ADD – FOLDER
15. A New Folder window will pop up where you can name your folder and enter a detailed description of its contents (ex: Maps)
16. Click OK.

17. Scroll down the Places Panel and you will see your new Maps folder
18. Look down further to the Temporary Places folder in the Places Panel. It will be open and contain a place that is checked. This is the 1915 San Francisco map you currently have overlaid on the globe.
19. Click, drag, and drop the map file into your Maps folder. The overlay can be turned on and off by clicking and unclicking the checkbox next to it.
20. Right-click the name of the map and select Rename. Call it "1915 San Francisco map."

You can follow this same process and save various Rumsey maps to your surname folders as well.

Creating Your Own Custom Historic Map Overlay

While Rumsey Historic Maps can be very useful in your research, unfortunately there are just a limited number available. It is very possible that there are no maps available for many of your ancestral locations. Don't worry... Rumsey Historical Maps are only the beginning.

Chances are at some point in your research you've come across a Land Plat Map for an area where an ancestor lived. If you were really fortunate your ancestor's name was included on the map indicating the parcel that they owned.

In fact, today there are literally hundreds of thousands of digital maps online and available for download. That means that there's a very good chance that somewhere out there is the map you are looking for. When you find that map, you can create your own custom historical map overlay in Google Earth!

Here's an example of a plat map from a county history book available in public libraries. It shows Wayne Township in Randolph County, Indiana as it was in 1882. Owners' names and the amount of acreage they own are indicated on the map. This map would be ideal for turning into a Google Earth overlay.

How to Create Your Own Historic Map Overlay:

Step One: *Digitize the Image*

The first step to creating your own historic map overlay is to convert the map to a digital image. In this case the map could be photocopied from the book, then scanned with a desktop scanner and saved as a JPEG picture file onto your computer's hard drive.

If you are fortunate enough to find a map like this online you can then just save the digital image to your computer by right clicking your mouse and saving it to a location of your choice on your hard drive.

Step Two: *Fly There*

Next, fly to the area where your map is from. In this example we would type Wayne, Randolph, Indiana in the Fly To box and click the Begin Search button.

Step Three: *Add Image Overlay*

There are two ways to add Image Overlays. Either method will open the New Image Overlay box and also add green crosshair markers to the map.

Method 1: Go up to the top menu bar and click the Image Overlay button (it looks like two pieces of paper overlaying each other)

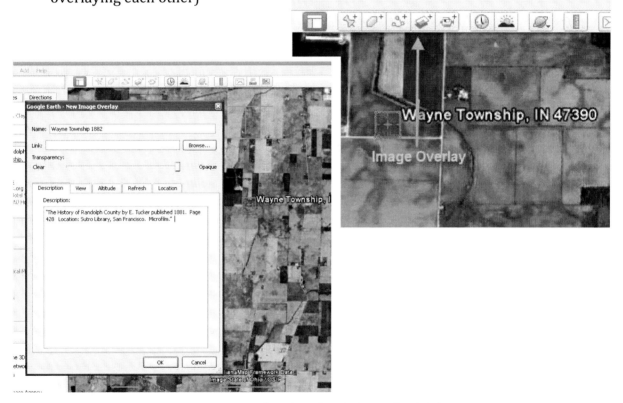

Method 2: Go to the Places Panel and right click on the folder you just created and select Add, then Image Overlay.

Step Four: *Name and Describe the Map*

You can name your historic map in the new Image Overlay box. (In this example I could use "Wayne Township 1882.")

The description area of the box is where you would type information about the source of the map. This is much like citing sources in your genealogy database. (You may even want to use standard source citation format in this box.)

For this example: "The History of Randolph County by E. Tucker published 1881. Page 428 Location: Sutro Library, San Francisco. Microfilm."

Step Five: *Attach the Map*

Attach the digital map image to this Overlay by clicking the Browse button and navigating your way to the location of the map on your computer hard drive.

Note: Do not click OK or close the Overlay box. It must remain open while you adjust the map.

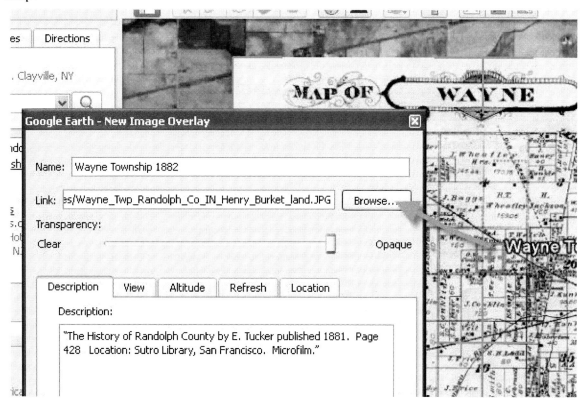

After a few moments the map will appear on the screen within the green placeholder lines.

> **QUICK TIP**: At this point you may want to hide the sidebar panel by clicking the Hide Sidebar button in the toolbar. This will give you more room to work. You can also grab and drag the Overlay box over to one side and even grab the corners of the box to make it a bit smaller, again providing more room to work.

Notice the Transparency slider tool in the Overlay box. Slide the lever to the right and your map will become more opaque. Slide it to the left and the map becomes transparent so that you can see the current landscape beneath the

historic map. This tool is critical for assisting you in sizing the map precisely to the modern day Google Earth map.

Step Six: *Matching Up Points*

Look for unique features on the historic map. What do you notice about this map of Wayne Township? Something that stands out is the very dark lines that merge together. These lines represent the railroad at that time. Look in the Wayne Township area on Google Earth to see if you can spot that railroad. Slide the transparency lever to the left to make the map transparent. Most locations have some type of distinct element that will help identify a starting point for positioning the map.

In this example we could use the point where the two railroad tracks intersect as a spot to match up with the historic map. By playing with the transparency tool back and forth you can see each map until you get the points you selected lined up together.

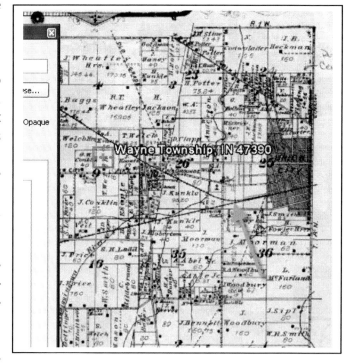

Step Seven: *Resizing the Map*

Once the maps have been lined up to match at that particular point, you'll probably notice that much of the rest of the map does not match up. That's because when you add the map it's not going to be exactly the same size as the Google Earth map. You will need to resize the overlay map until everything lines up.

You'll notice that when you hover your mouse over a green cross-hair line the hand icon turns into a pointer finger. This means that you can grab that spot and manipulate just the overlay. If you hover your mouse over the map in an area without a green line your mouse pointer is an entire hand and that means that you'll be moving the entire map – Google Earth and your overlay together. To resize just the overlay to match up with Google Earth go to a corner and grab the green line and pull the overlay. Play with it, pulling the various corners until all the landmarks line up.

In this example we have railroad lines and a number of rivers to work with. Zoom out to give yourself enough of the Google Earth map to work with. Keep using the Transparency tool to continue checking your progress. The goal is to line up all of the landmarks throughout the map. Things may look lined up with the railroad, but the river in another corner could still be out of alignment. But in the end, if the historic map you are working with is accurate, it should line up beautifully with Google Earth. Then when you use the Transparency Lever you can really see what the land of your ancestors many, many years ago looks today.

Step Eight: *File Management*
Locate the map overlay you created and drag and drop it into the appropriate file folder in the Places Panel.

Step Nine: *Set the Transparency Level*
Before you click OK and close the map overlay box, drag the Transparency Lever all the way to the right so that your map is completely opaque. Then click OK.

Now you can see your map on Google Earth. But what if you don't want it always to be visible? To make the historic map transparent, go to the Places Panel and slide the Transparency Lever at the bottom of the panel to adjust the transparency of the map you are displaying on Google
Earth. If you want to turn this overlay off so that it is invisible, uncheck the box for the map overlay in the Places Panel and it will disappear. To make it visible, just click the box.

Try it For Yourself:
Create Your First Custom Historic Map Overlay

Select a map from your genealogy research and create an historic map overlay in Google Earth following the nine steps above. If you don't have any old maps, locate one for one of your ancestral locations from any of the following websites that collectively hold more than 385,000 digitized maps from the U.S. and around the world:

American Memory Map Collections at the Library of Congress
http://lcweb2.loc.gov/ammem/gmdhtml/

British Library
http://www.bl.uk/onlinegallery/onlineex/mapsviews/index.html

Hargrett Rare Book & Manuscript Library
http://www.libs.uga.edu/darchive/hargrett/maps/maps.html

National Library of Australia
http://sbdsproto.nla.gov.au/sbdp-ui/island/map

Perry-Castaneda Library Map Collection
http://www.lib.utexas.edu/maps/

Visual Collections (including the David Rumsey Collection)
http://www.davidrumsey.com/collections/cartography.html

QUICK TIP: How to Find Plat Maps Online
1. Go to www.Google.com
2. Click the Images link in the upper left corner
3. Click the Advanced Search link to the right of the search box
4. Enter keywords in the Find Results search fields
5. Under Content Types select Line Drawings
6. Click the Google Search Button
7. Refine your search as necessary to home in on the map you need

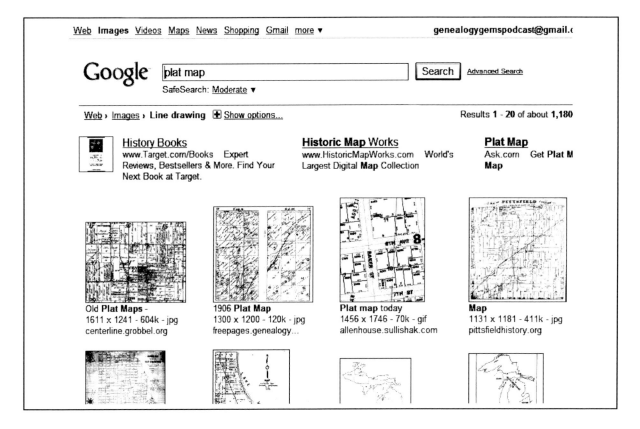

Additional Reading: Learn more about plat maps
http://en.wikipedia.org/wiki/Plat

Saving and Sharing Custom Historic Map Overlays

While the maps that you create are temporarily saved to your computer hard drive nested within the Google Earth system folders, they can be a challenge to locate and may even be stored as hidden files on your computer.

If you want to save your historic map overlays that you create and share them with others, it is recommended that you save them to a folder of your choosing that is easy to locate and work with.

Places are saved in a unique geographic format called KML. When you add an overlay or other files and save it, you are creating a zipped KMZ file folder. When opened these files automatically launch Google Earth and display in the 3D Viewer.

How to Save Your Map Overlay to Your Computer:

1. Go up to the Google Earth menu and click File – Save – Save Place As and the Save File box will pop up
2. Click the down arrow of the Where field and navigate to where you want to save your file on your computer's hard drive
3. Click Save
4. Go to your computer's hard drive (i.e. Mac: Finder, Windows: Explorer) and locate the file you just saved

As we discussed, it is possible to share your KMZ files. You can:

- E-mail them (right-click the file in the Places panel and select Email. The KMZ file will be automatically attached to the email)
- Host them locally for sharing within a private Internet
- Host them publicly on a web server

Just as web browsers display HTML files, Earth browsers such as Google Earth display KMZ files. If you're technically inclined and you decide you want to share your KMZ file online, it's just important to know that the KMZ zipped file folder must be opened and the contents extracted for them to be available on your website for use. But once you've had them uploaded properly to your website, you can share the URL address of your KML files on your website and anyone who has Google Earth installed can download and view your maps.

Where Google Earth and the Census Intersect

Historic maps are powerful tools for gaining deeper insight into the lives of your ancestors. Imagine the possibilities when your genealogical records, such as the census, intersect with Google Earth and your historic map overlays!

To illustrate this let's take a closer look at Henry Burkett's farm on the Wayne Co., Indiana plat map.

A great thing about plat maps is that they may list not only your ancestor but all of his neighbors (who may also possibly be relatives) as well. That's where maps and census records intersect beautifully.

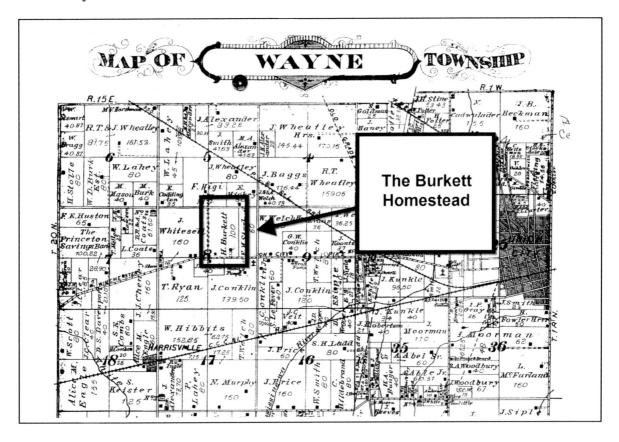

Since this example plat map is dated 1882, we would want to pull up the 1880 census record showing Henry and his family living in Wayne Township.

In this case we can see that Jacob Conklin is listed just a little further down the census page.

On the map the census comes to life as we see J. Conklin with 139 and ½ acres across the road. While the census can tell us the names of neighbors, it is only in combination with this historic map that the neighborhood comes into real perspective.

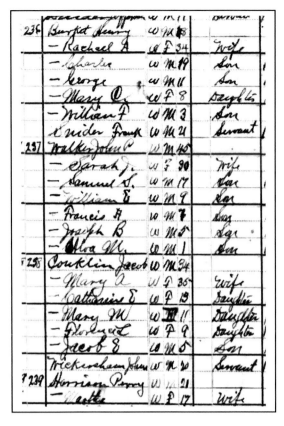

Keep in mind that some of the folks who look like neighbors on the census are actually living on someone else's property and therefore may not be named on the map.

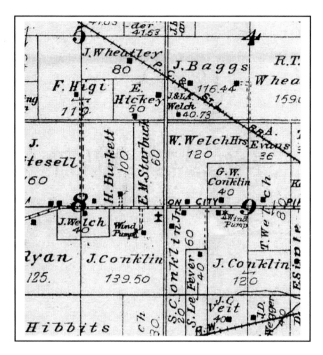

Perry Harrison, listed after the Conklin family, names his occupation as "Works on Farm" versus his neighbors who are listed as Farmer. So it is not a big surprise that Perry Harrison is not listed on the plat map because he's likely renting a place and working as hired farm labor. For the Harrison descendants, using the plat map in conjunction with the census goes a long way in helping them identify the location where Perry and his wife Martha lived even though they were not land owners.

Going Visiting

Incorporating Street View can add an additional layer to the map and census that allows you to "visit" your ancestor and his census neighbors! Let's use our Wayne Township neighborhood again for this example.

Step 1:
Make this map overlay more transparent by moving the Transparency Lever in the Places panel to the left so that you can see Google Earth behind it. Click and drag the Street View icon and drop it onto the map.

Step 2:

Blue lines will appear on the roads where Street View is available.

Step 3:

Zoom in closer to the farm in question. In this case we can now see the house and barn that stand on the property today. These could very likely be the same buildings that stood there when the Burkett's lived there in 1882.

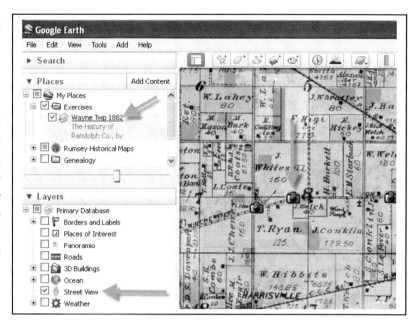

Step 4:

Exit street view by clicking Exit Photo in the top right corner of the screen.

Step 5:

To obtain the current address for the property today hover your mouse over the icon nearest the house and Google Earth will display the address.

When it comes to getting up close and personal with your ancestors, the sky's the limit with Google Earth!

CHAPTER 17
Google Earth – Plotting Your Ancestor's Homestead

In this chapter we are going to experience how Google Earth can interact with other online websites and tools to help you explore the land your ancestors once inhabited.

Plotting An Ancestor's Homestead

In the United States, Land Patents document the transfer of land ownership from the federal government to individuals. It is very likely that at some point in your research you will come across an ancestor who received a Land Patent.

You may already be familiar with the Bureau of Land Management's General Federal Land Records website at www.glorecords.blm.gov. This is the first place you would search online for an ancestor's Land Patent Record.

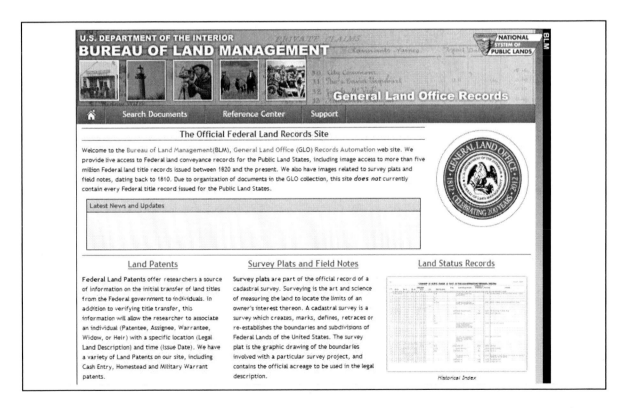

The Bureau of Land Management's General Federal Land Records website is where you can access Federal land conveyance records for the Public Land States. This website provides image access to more than three million Federal Land title records for Eastern Public Land States issued between 1820 and 1908. The site is also adding images of Military Land Warrants, which were issued to individuals as a reward for their military service. However, be aware that the site still does not contain every Federal title record issued for the Public Land States. If you don't find a record you are looking for, you will need to pursue other conventional sources.

According to the Bureau of Land Management:

"The authority of many acts of Congress - sale, homesteads, disposed of the land military warrants for military service, timber culture, mining, etc. One of the primary purposes of these public land laws was to encourage people from the East to move west. In the early 1800s people could buy public land for $1.25 an acre. For a time, they could buy up to 640 acres under this law. The sale of public land under the "Cash Act" is no longer in effect.

Several Military Warrant Acts granted public land to soldiers instead of pay. These acts have been repealed.

The Homestead Act of 1862 allowed people to settle up to 160 acres of public land if they lived on it for five years and grew crops or made improvements. This land did not cost anything per acre, but the settler did pay a filing fee. This act is no longer in effect."

How to Search the BLM website:

1. Click Search Land Patents from the menu

2. Select the state where you believe they owned the land

3. Enter the Last name

4. Enter the first name

5. Click Search

Here is an example of search results.

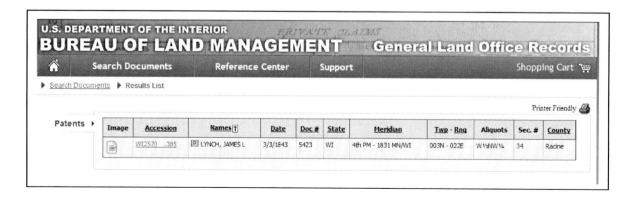

Click on the Image icon to view the original Land Patent image.

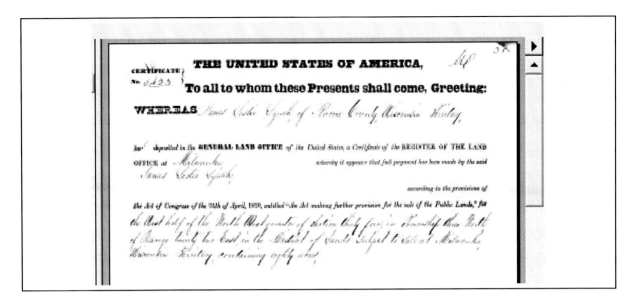

QUICK TIP: Saving and Printing Land Patents
The best way to print or save a quality land patent image is to click the Document Image tab and select PDF.

Chances are if you have searched for records on this website before, you may have stopped at this point because you located the record you were looking for. However, with Google Earth you can make even more use of the valuable information provided on this website.

Land Patent Details

Notice that in addition to the button that accesses the digitized image of the land patent, the name of the patentee is hyperlinked. Clicking on the linked name of your ancestor will bring you to the Land Patent Details page.

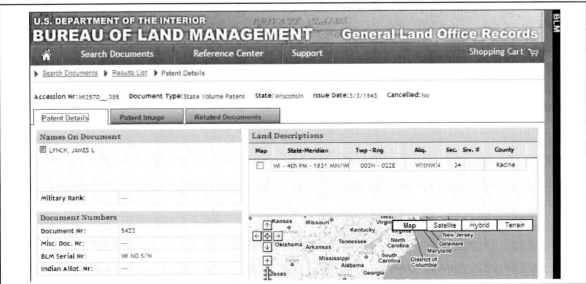

There are four tabs of information about this Land Patent record. The Patent Description tab provides transcribed details from the original record. The Document Image Tab gives you more options in regards to downloading the original image. And the Legal Land Description tab provides specific geographic data that we can use to plot this Land Patent on Google Earth.

Image Below: Legal Land Description

Map	State-Meridian	Twp - Rng	Aliq.	Sec.	Srv. #	County
☐	WI - 4th PM - 1831 MN/WI	003N - 022E	W½NW¼	34		Racine

Land Descriptions

This description gives us the exact coordinates of the property. However, most of us are not prepared to use this type of data. That's where a website called EarthPoint comes in at www.earthpoint.us.

This website was created by Bill Clark who is sharing his geographic expertise in terrific ways. The site is free, though there are some paid subscription features. But plotting your ancestor's land patent is free.

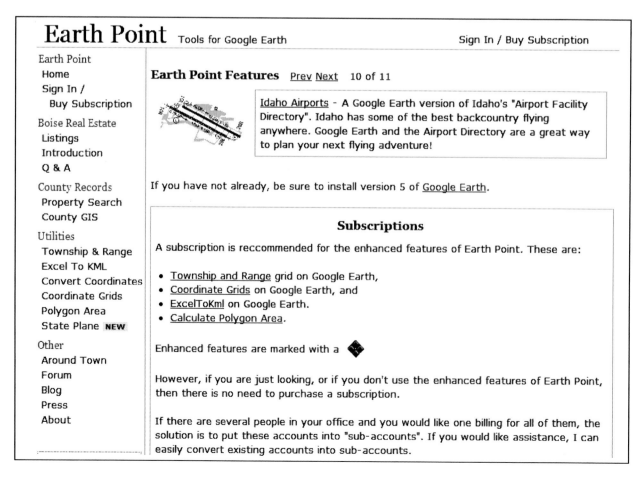

Earth Point Tools for Google Earth   Sign In / Buy Subscription

Earth Point
Home
Sign In /
 Buy Subscription

Boise Real Estate
Listings
Introduction
Q & A

County Records
Property Search
County GIS

Utilities
Township & Range
Excel To KML
Convert Coordinates
Coordinate Grids
Polygon Area
State Plane NEW

Other
Around Town
Forum
Blog
Press
About

Earth Point Features Prev Next   10 of 11

Idaho Airports - A Google Earth version of Idaho's "Airport Facility Directory". Idaho has some of the best backcountry flying anywhere. Google Earth and the Airport Directory are a great way to plan your next flying adventure!

If you have not already, be sure to install version 5 of Google Earth.

Subscriptions

A subscription is reccommended for the enhanced features of Earth Point. These are:

- Township and Range grid on Google Earth,
- Coordinate Grids on Google Earth, and
- ExcelToKml on Google Earth.
- Calculate Polygon Area.

Enhanced features are marked with a ◆

However, if you are just looking, or if you don't use the enhanced features of Earth Point, then there is no need to purchase a subscription.

If there are several people in your office and you would like one billing for all of them, the solution is to put these accounts into "sub-accounts". If you would like assistance, I can easily convert existing accounts into sub-accounts.

How to Plot An Ancestor's Land Patent:

1. Go to www.glorecords.blm.gov
2. Pull up the Land Patent Details in one browser window
3. In a second browser window go to www.earthpoint.us
4. Click on the Township and Range link in the menu column
5. Scroll down to where it says "Convert Township, Range, and Section to Latitude and Longitude"
6. Select the state
7. Using the data from the Land Patent Details, Select the Principal Meridian
8. Select the Township
9. Select the Range
10. Select the Section
11. Click the Fly to On Google Earth button

Image Below: Earthpoint has plotted land from the Legal Description in Google Earth

QUICK TIP: Enter Data in the Order Requested
Start with the top item which is State and enter each piece of information from the legal description into the appropriate field, in order, and allow a few seconds for it to register your selection. Each selection will determine the next drop menu.

Convert Township, Range, and Section to Latitude and Longitude

Enter Township and Range. Optionally enter Section. Google Earth flys you there using BLM data. Hint: pause for a moment after choosing each of the criteria. This allows the data to be loaded into the drop-down boxes.

State | Wisconsin ▼
Principal Meridian | Fourth ▼
Township | 003 N ▼
Range | 022 E ▼
Section | 034 ▼

[View]   Free. User account is not needed.

[Fly To On Google Earth]   If you want to see the surrounding townships, then once you have clicked the "Fly To" button, come back and click the BLM or National Atlas "View on Google Earth" button. Free. User account is not needed.

Clicking the Fly to On Google Earth button on the Earthpoint web page will automatically open and launch the Google Earth program on your computer. It will zoom directly to the place on the map where the land is located.

The Township is outlined in orange, and the Section is outlined in purple. We are now looking at the exact piece of property that was described on the original land patent record! Notice that in the smaller purple square there is a purple ball marking the exact center. Click that and a dialogue box will pop up providing a complete description of the property.

Image At Right: Legal Land Description Plotted in Google Earth. Large Square Outline is the township, and the small square at the bottom of the township is the section.

Section | S34 T3N R22E
Meridian | Fourth
State | Wisconsin
Source | USFS

Calculated Values
Acres | 642
Centroid | 42.6760549, -87.8849202
Corners | NW 42.6834319, -87.8947642
| NE 42.6831320, -87.8750642
| SE 42.6687220, -87.8750543
| SW 42.6690045, -87.8948217

For illustration only. User to verify all information. www.earthpoint.us

How to Virtually Visit and Mark the "Old Homestead":

1. Search for a land patent
2. View the original record
3. View the Land Patent Details for that record
4. Plot the Land Patent using Earthpoint in conjunction with Google Earth
5. Activate Street View
6. Zoom back out so that you can see the entire purple square outlining the Section
7. Go back to the BLM website and pull up the original Land Patent by clicking the index card button next to the patentee's name
8. Find the handwritten description of the exact piece of property that the Patentee received (ex: "The West half of the NW Quarter of section 34")
9. Note how many acres were received
10. Go to http://www.genealogygems.tv/Pages/Store/VolII_Bonus_Content.htm and download the free acreage image that suits the property, or create your own in a graphic program
11. Go back to Google Earth
12. The Section is outlined in purple. Click the ball in the center and find out the total acreage of the section
13. Locate the property according to the land patent description

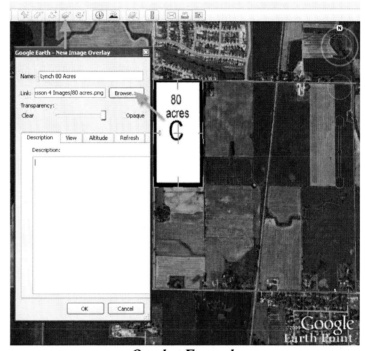

Overlay Example

14. To delineate the acreage you have two options:
    *   Click the Add Image Overlay, import the acreage image you downloaded from the link above, and resize the image overlay to fit. Fill in the Title and Description and click OK
    *   Click the Add Polygon button on the toolbar. Click in the upper left corner of the acreage, and then click the upper right and so on until the property is outlined. Click the Style, Color tab and select yellow, and make the Width of the line 2.5. Fill in the Title and Description and click OK.

Polygon Example

15. Notice that the overlay or polygon appears in the Places panel. Move the overlay or path into the appropriate folder.
16. Activate Street View
17. Zoom in on the buildings on the property and investigate them with Street View. Which one do you think is most likely to have been the site of the original home? What is the nearby address of that location?
18. When finished, click the EXIT Window button.

Get to Know the Community

Just as we got to know the neighbors of Henry Burkett from the census on the plat map, it can be very interesting to visit the neighboring community of rural areas where our ancestors owned property. What's it like today? Are there examples of architecture still standing from that era? To find out, zoom out a bit farther and look for a nearby town, then zoom in with Street View to see what it's like.

QUICK TIP: Spotting Older Neighborhoods
A quick way to spot the older neighborhoods in a nearby town that may have examples of the older architecture is to look at the street layouts. Newer neighborhoods often have curves and cul-de-sacs. Older neighborhoods tend to be laid out in a grid pattern with few dead-end streets.

So there you have it. You have another way to look more in-depth at the land your ancestors settled. Now you don't have to wait for good airfares. You can visit your ancestor's homesteads yourself with Google Earth.

CHAPTER 18
Google Earth – Fun with Images & Video

As you discover exciting new ways to view your family history at some point you will want to share your findings with others: your family, other researchers, or the world at large! The good news is that with Google Earth you can, and in some very interesting and creative ways.

In the previous chapters we explored how the census can intersect with Google Earth. But the census is just one genealogical document associated with locations. Consider virtually visiting:

- the church where your ancestors worshipped (church records)
- the cemetery where they are buried (burial records)
- the photographer's studio where they got their portrait taken (old photos)
- the businesses where they worked (social security records)
- the distant locations where they fought in wars (military records)
- the schools they attended (educational records)

...and the list goes on.

In this chapter we will incorporate your virtual visits to these locations into images, videos, and tours that will bring it all together in a unique collage of your family history that you can share with others.

Genealogical Images in Placemarks

Chances are that you not only have copies of documents in the categories listed above, but also old family photos depicting some of those locations. Any type of digital image can be incorporated into a Placemark. You can mark the spot and click the Placemark to view the associated images. Best of all, you can incorporate as many Placemarks as you would like.

How to Add an Image to a Placemark:

1. Upload the image to the Internet
   a. Your own website
   b. A commercial website such as www.Photobucket.com (free)

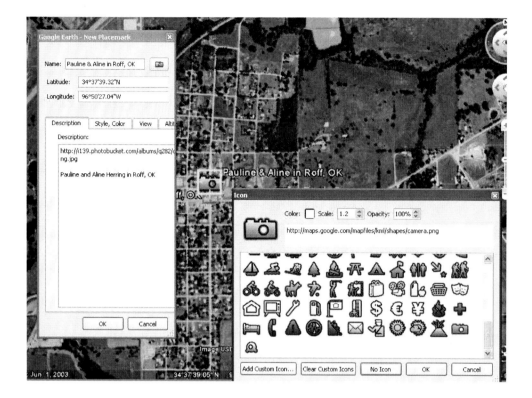

2. In Google Earth fly to the location where you want to place an image
3. Click the Placemark button in the toolbar
4. Click and drag the placemark to the exact location on the map
5. Type a name for the Placemark in the New Placemark box
6. Copy the URL address for the image if it is hosted on your own site. In the Description area of the New Placemark box type the example Image Code (below) including the URL address that you copied.
    a. Example: **<IMG src=**"http://www.yoursite.com/yourphoto.jpg**">**
    b. Note: Any website address where your image resides can be inserted in the above code. The code in **bold** must remain the same.
    c. Sites like Photobucket automatically generate the code for you so all you have to do is copy it. Just hover your mouse over your uploaded image and copy the IMG CODE. Or you can click the Share link above the image to obtain the code.

Image in Photobucket

7. Under the image code you can type text to accompany your image
8. Click the Style / Color tab if you would like to change the color of the Placemark text in the 3D Viewer
    a. Under Label click the color square and select a color
9. Click the pushpin icon to the right of the Placemark name at the top of the window Select the camera icon to represent a photograph and click OK
10. Click OK to finish and close the Placemark window

Now when you click on the Placemark the photo appears in the Placemark dialogue box.

You may decide after adding some Placemarks that you would like to make some adjustments to them. Here's how:

How to Rename a Placemark:

1. Go to the Places panel
2. Right-click the Placemark name
3. Select Rename
4. Type in a new name
5. Click OK

How to Revise a Placemark:

1. Go to the Places panel
2. Right-click the Placemark name
3. Select Properties
4. Edit the Placemark window
5. Click OK to finish

Adding Videos to Google Earth Maps

As with images, videos can also be incorporated into your maps in Google Earth. Whether you want to include a simple home movie or an elaborate documentary-style commentary, you can do so with Placemarks. Don't worry if you don't know how or don't want to create your own video. There are thousands of free videos available on websites such as YouTube that can tremendously enhance your maps and exploration of your family history.

Image Below: Video uploaded to YouTube.com

How to Add a Video to a Placemark:

1. Upload the Video to a free Video hosting website
   a. www.YouTube.com
   b. http://video.google.com
2. Copy the embed code for the video
3. In Google Earth fly to the location where you want to place the video
4. Click the Placemark button in the toolbar
5. Click and drag the placemark to the exact location
6. Type a name for the Placemark in the New Placemark box
7. Paste the video embed code into the Description area of the New Placemark box
8. Under the code you can type text to accompany your video if you wish
9. Click the Style / Color tab if you would like to change the color of the Placemark text in the 3D Viewer

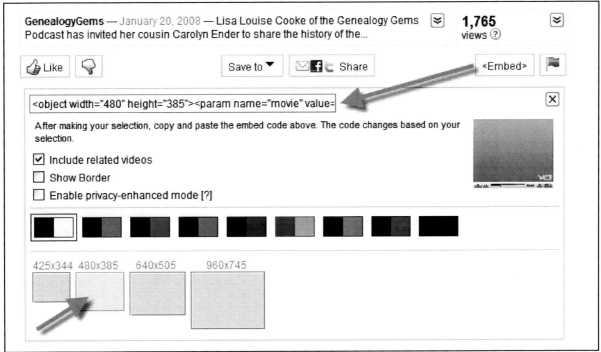

GenealogyGems — January 20, 2008 — Lisa Louise Cooke of the Genealogy Gems
Podcast has invited her cousin Carolyn Ender to share the history of the...

1,765 views ?

Like   Save to ▾   Share   <Embed>

<object width="480" height="385"><param name="movie" value=

After making your selection, copy and paste the embed code above. The code changes based on your selection.

☑ Include related videos
☐ Show Border
☐ Enable privacy-enhanced mode [?]

425x344   480x385   640x505   960x745

Image Above: Copy the Video Embed Code

    a.   Under Label click the color square and select a color
10. To change the placemark icon image, click the pushpin icon to the right of the Placemark name at the top of the window
11. Select the movie projector or TV set icon to represent video and click OK
12. Click OK to finish and close the Placemark window

As promised, you don't have to create your own video in order to enhance your Google Earth maps with compelling video.

Herring Quilting Heritage

Genealogy Gems Presents: Heritage Quilts

0:00 / 6:56

YouTube

The Herrings of Roff, Oklahoma held a long tradition of quilting. Watch this video to see an example of the family history sewn into a quilt.
Directions: To here - From here

Image Left: Click the placemark icon to reveal the video in the popup dialogue box. You must be connected to the Internet in order to play the video.

Try It For Yourself:
How to Add Existing Video to a Google Earth Map

1. In Google Earth fly to the historic seaside town of Margate, Kent, England
2. Open your Internet browser and go to www.youtube.com
3. In the search box type Margate History and click the Search button
4. Click on the video Margate Sea Front 1890 – 1903. This video is a compelling presentation of historic images set to music. (If you don't see this video in the list search on the exact title. If you do not locate this video, feel free to select another from your Margate History search result list.)
5. Select the color and size for the video player. (Smaller players are recommended so they don't cover too much of the map while playing.)
6. After making your selection, copy the embed code. (Note: The code changes based on your player selections.)
7. Go back to your Margate map in Google Earth
8. Click the Placemark button in the toolbar
9. Click and drag the placemark to the center of Margate if needed
10. Type "Margate 1890 – 1930" as the name for the Placemark in the New Placemark box.
11. Paste the video embed code into the Description area of the New Placemark box
12. Press the Enter key on your keyboard to go to the next line and type the text "Watch the video tour of Margate, Kent 1890 to 1930."
13. Click the Style / Color tab
14. Click the color square and a blue color
15. Click the pushpin icon to the right of the Placemark name at the top of the window
16. Select the movie projector icon to represent video and click OK
17. Click OK to finish and close the Placemark window
18. In the Places panel, click and drag the placemark into the folder of your choice.
19. Click on the Placemark on your map to open the dialogue box
20. Click and watch the video!

QUICK TIP: Color Coding
Consider making all photograph placemarks one particular color and all video placemarks another color. A consistent color-coding scheme makes it quick and easy for viewers to find what they are looking for on your Google Earth map, particularly if you have included a large amount of content.

Focusing in on an Area

Since the goal for this content is to share it with others, it can be very helpful to provide indicators for your user as to the area you want them to focus on by outlining it. An outline or border can be created with the Polygon tool found in the toolbar.

How to Outline An Area of Focus:

1. Fly back to Margate, England or to an area pertinent to your family history that you wish to focus on
2. Click the Polygon tool in the toolbar
3. Click in the upper left corner of the area on the map you want to border
4. Click the upper right corner
5. Click the lower left corner completing a rectangle border
6. Hover your mouse over a corner and the mouse pointer, which is currently a square polygon tool, becomes a hand tool allowing you to click on the corners and drag them to adjust the size and shape of your polygon
7. In the New Polygon box name your polygon "Family History Focus Area"
8. Click the Style / Color tab
9. Under the Area section click the drop down box and select Outline
10. Under the Lines section select the color you want the border to be
11. Increase the Width of the border to 3.0
12. Click OK to finish

Image Below: Outlining an Area of Focus on the Map

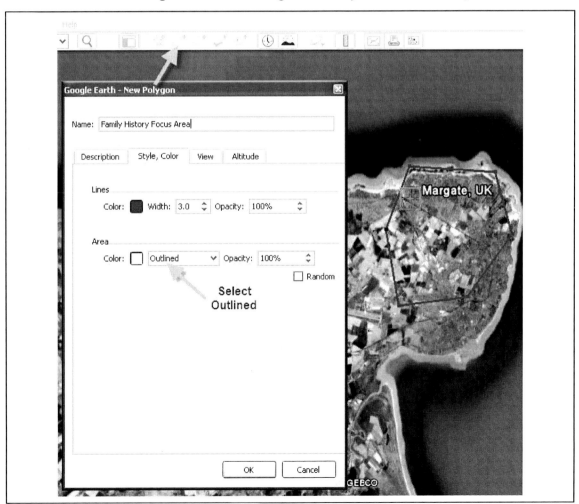

Recording a Family History Tour

At this point it's easy to imagine adding a variety of Placemarks to an area on the globe where your ancestors once lived: videos, photos, documents, etc. Once you have compiled so much interesting content you can share it with your family, friends, and fellow researchers by recording your own tour of the area.

Before you get started, it's best to jot down some notes for yourself about what you want to cover in the tour. For a really smooth presentation consider writing a script.

The Record A Tour button looks like a video camera and is located on the Google Earth toolbar. When clicked a small recording panel will appear in the bottom left corner of the 3D Viewer. You have two recording options:

1. Click the red Record button and only the screen will be recorded
2. Click the microphone button and the screen and audio will be recorded.

Typically if you have a microphone built in to your computer, it will be recording the audio. However, you can also plug in an external microphone into your computer.

How to Record A Family History Tour:

1. Fly to the location where you want to begin your tour
2. Click the Record a Tour button on the toolbar
3. A small recording panel will appear in the bottom left corner of the 3D viewer
4. Press the red Record or Microphone button (depending on whether or not you wish to record audio as well) and navigate the map as you wish for it to be seen in the recording, highlighting Placemarks and other noteworthy content
5. When finished pause a few seconds and then click the red button again to stop
6. The recorded tour will automatically begin to play back
7. Click the Save button on the player and a New Tour window will open
8. Type a name for the tour
9. Type a description of what the tour will show the viewer
10. Click OK
11. The saved tour now appears in your Places panel
12. Click and drag the tour into your Exercises folder if it is not already there
13. Click the tour in the Places panel to play it again

To stop recording press the red button again. The tour will play back automatically to show you the results and the recording panel will convert to a media player.

QUICK TIP: Recording
Let the recorder run a few extra seconds after you have finished before you stop the recording. This will ensure that your recording is not cut short prematurely as Google Earth can sometimes shave a few seconds off the recording.

As a tour plays, the viewer can look around by clicking and dragging the view. This is not the same as navigating Google Earth because you can only look around from the viewpoints of the tour. When you pause a tour, you can then navigate anywhere you want. When you click the play button again, the tour resumes where it left off.

Once you have recorded your tour and reviewed it, be sure to click the Save Tour button. A New Tour window will pop up allowing you to name and describe your tour. The saved tour will then appear in your Places panel.

QUICK TIP: Highlighting Video Content in a Tour
If you click on a placemark that contains a video don't attempt to play it during the recording, as it will not appear that way in the recorded tour. It is better to demonstrate to your viewer that the video is available and they can play the video right from the tour view if they wish. Keep in mind that you are recording a "Tour" which is a geographic KML file, not a true standard "Video," and therefore you are not "screen capturing."

Sharing and Saving Tours

In the next section of this chapter you will learn how to share all of the content you have created with others. The content will be combined together and saved as a KMZ file. However, before we get to that there's one more bit of business to take care of.

Adding a Virtual Tour Guide Placemark

Because Video Tours aren't marked on the map with an icon like a Placemark, it's recommended that you create a custom Placemark to alert your intended user to the existence of the Tour within the KMZ file.

How to Create a Virtual Tour Placemark:

1. Fly to the general area where your recorded tour takes place
2. Click the Add Placemark button in the toolbar
3. Move the placemark on the screen to a location where it doesn't interfere with other content but can be easily found
4. In the Add Placemark box type the title "Virtual Tour"

5. In the Description box type the following instructions for your user: "In the Places panel click the plus sign next to this KMZ file and select the TOUR to watch the recorded tour I created for you."
6. Click the pushpin icon next to the name in the Placemark box
7. Click the Add Custom Icon button at the bottom of the box
8. Select an image that represents the tour or use the one I've created for you on this page: http://www.genealogygems.tv/Pages/Store/VolII_Bonus_Content.htm
9. At the top of the Icon window increase the Scale to 2.0 so that the Tour Guide icon will stand out, and click OK.
10. Click OK to close the Placemark box.
11. Click on the Tour Guide icon on your map and a dialogue box will pop up providing instructions on how to access the recorded tour you created.

Image Below: Adding a Virtual Tour Icon

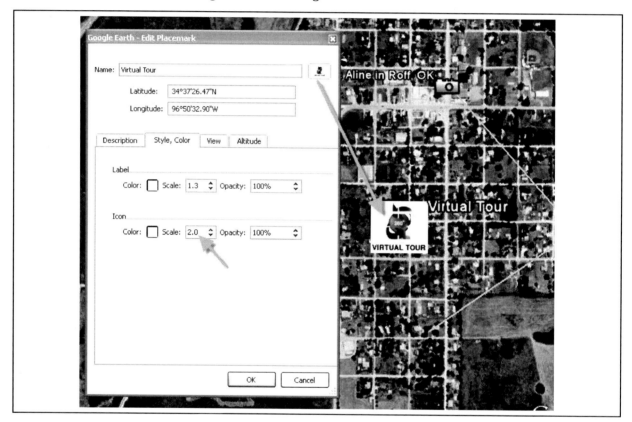

Now you your content is ready to save and share with others!

Saving Content Rich Family History Maps

When you have finished creating the family history Placemarks and Tours you will need to pull them all together in order to save and share them.

How to Save Your Family History Map:

1. Go to the Places panel
2. Right Click on the My Places Folder and select Add and Folder
3. Name your new folder
   a. Example: Smith Family History
4. Drag and drop each content item you created into the new folder (Photos and Video Placemarks, Tour Guide, etc.)
5. Photos and Video Placemarks, Tour Guide, etc.
6. After you have added all of the content you want to include, right-click the folder and select Save Place As
7. In the pop up window name the file as desired, and save it to your desktop
   a. Note: Leave the file type as KMZ
8. Click OK
9. Close Google Earth
10. Go to your computer's desktop
11. Click on KMZ file you just created which will automatically re-launch Google Earth and display all of the saved content.
12. Click on the various content icons to test them.

QUICK TIP: What You See Is What You Get

Keep in mind that any layers you have activated at the time you create and save your files will appear in the final KMZ file. For instance, if you have Borders and Labels activated, or Discovery Networks (in the Gallery folder) activated, those icons are going to appear as well which might clutter and confuse the view for your user. It's best to de-activate any layers not directly pertaining to the family history view you wish to share before saving it.

Sharing Content Rich Family History Maps

Now that your family history content is neatly packaged into a KMZ file it's ready to be sent to family, friends and fellow researchers. The easiest way to do that is to email it.

Simply open your preferred email program, create a new email message, and attach the KMZ file that you saved to your desktop. When the recipient opens the file it will automatically launch in Google Earth (providing they have Google Earth installed on their computer).

QUICK TIP: Make It Easy on Recipients

Consider including a link to the Google Earth download page in your email for the folks who receive your emailed KMZ family history files. For example: "Download Google Earth for free at http://earth.google.com/". That way they can easily download the free program before launching your file.

Conclusion

Storytelling is an important piece of the genealogical puzzle. A good story is hard for even the non-genealogist to resist. Now with Google Earth you will be able to create and share compelling stories of your family history.

CHAPTER 19
Family History Tour Maps

Geographic locations are a critical part of genealogical research. Maps can reveal patterns, terrain obstacles, and other key factors that can help you better understand your ancestors' lives and know where the next logical place to look for clues would be. By pulling together all of the elements you've been working with so far, you can create what I like to call a *Family History Tour Map* that you can share with your family and use as a powerful reference tool in your research. You can customize and create your own maps in the Places panel and save them to your computer. You can even record a tour of your map for sharing.

Let's talk about the components of a *Family History Tour Map*. Some of the things you can include are:

- Custom placemark icons representing life events at various locations (births, school, marriage, residences, ports of immigration, deaths)
- Photos
- Additional text and stories
- Paths of movements
- Overlays of historic maps and images
- 3D Models of homes and other significant items

A Family History Tour Map tells a story. Here are some ideas for tours you may want to create:
- The life of an ancestor
- Migration
- Catastrophic events
- Ancestors' work history
- 2 families that join through marriage
- History of a village

All of the elements of the map will be saved to one folder within the Places panel. Begin by creating that folder.

How to Create a Family History Tour Map Folder:

1. Open the Places Panel
2. Click on My Places
3. Right click on My Places and select ADD – Folder
4. Name the folder (e.g. John Smith Life Tour)
5. Type additional details describing the tour into the description box if desired
6. Click OK

The new folder now resides in your My Places folder and its checkbox will be checked which means you are currently working on and viewing the contents of this folder. Each step from this point will be saved to this folder.

How to Add Life Event Icons to the Map:

1. Fly to the location where the life event occurred
2. Click the Push Pin icon on the toolbar
3. A New Placemark box will appear
4. Type in a name for the event in the Name field
5. Enter a detailed description or story in the Description tab
6. Click the icon button in the top right corner of the box to reveal an assortment of icons
7. Click the icon that best represents the life event, or add an icon to the Custom Icon Gallery. (If you need additional icons try a Google Image search. You can access the Web anytime while in Google Earth by selecting TOOLS – WEB from the menu)
8. Adjust the color, scale, and opacity of the icon at the top of the box if desired
9. Click OK

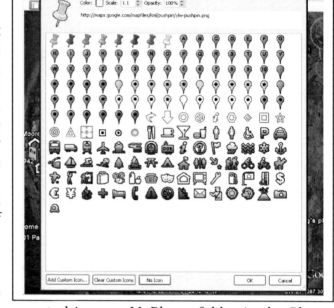

The Life Event now appears in the Family History Tour Map folder that you created in your MyPlaces folder in the Places Panel.

How to Add a Photo to a Life Event Icon:

The simplest way to add photos to your maps is to host your photos on a photo sharing website that automatically generates the html code you will need. For this example we are using www.Photobucket.com.

1. Upload your photo to Photobucket
2. Hover your mouse over the image to review the drop down box
3. Click the HTML code field and the code will automatically be copied
4. Open your map in Google Earth
5. Right click the icon that you want to associate the photograph with to open the Edit Placemark box
6. Paste the HTML code into the Description field
7. Add additional text or story if desired
8. Click OK
9. Click on the icon and the image and text will appear in a viewing box

Indicate Migration with Paths

You can draw free-form paths on your map to represent the movements of your ancestors and save them in you're My Places folder just like you did with the Life Event Icons. Paths share all of the features of placemarks (life event icons) including name, description, style view, and location. Once you create a path, you can play a tour of it.

How to Add a Path:

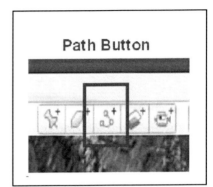

1. Mark the locations you want to use to create your path
2. Zoom in to your map as close as you can while still being able to see all of the locations.
3. Click the Path button on the toolbar
4. The New Path box will appear and the cursor will change to a square drawing tool
5. Enter the name and description of the path
6. Click the Style tab
7. Click the color box to pick the color of the path on the map
8. Select the desired width of the path line from the Width drop down menu
9. Click on the locations in the order of the life events (birth to death, or town of origin to Ellis Island to their new home in America.)
10. When complete click OK on the New Path box

How to Save A Family History Tour Map:

1. When you have added all of the desired elements to your map, go to the menu and select FILE –> SAVE –> SAVE PLACE AS
2. Name the map in the SAVE FILE box
3. Navigate to the place on your computer hard drive where you want to save the map
4. Click the Save button

Record a Tour of Your Ancestor's Family History Tour Map

Google Earth enables you to take viewers on a Family History Tour with the Record a Tour feature. Having a headset with microphone is ideal for recording a tour. If you want to narrate the tour, it's also very helpful to write out a basic script indicating the order in which your will navigate the locations and things of interest you wish to discuss.

How to Record a Family History Map Tour:

1. Start with the globe in a position to show you the tour's starting place and enough of the landscape for your viewers to get a perspective on the location

2. Click on the camera on the top menu to reveal the recording box in the lower left corner of the viewer

3. Click the Red circle record button if you want to record only your movements. Click the microphone button if you want to record narration with your tour

4. Once you click the Microphone button the counter will begin, which tells you that you are recording

5. Navigate your way from location to location, clicking Life Event icons to reveal photos and text

6. When you are done click the red Record button to stop

7. The Record controls will disappear and a "Play Control Bar" will automatically appear in the bottom left corner and the tour will begin to play

8. To save your recorded tour click the SAVE icon button on the right end of the play control bar, which will open a New Tour box

9. Name the recorded tour

10. Type in a description if desired

11. Click OK

12. You will see the name of your saved tour recording in the Places Panel with the check box checked. You can move the recording to any folder you wish within you're My Places folder by clicking, dragging, and dropping the title to the desired folder.

See It In Action!
VIDEO: *Google Earth Tour Creation Video*
http://www.youtube.com/watch?v=nuJwarqTLQA

www.GenealogyGems.com

Keys to Success

- Remember that the images, placemarks, and overlays you are seeing on the globe are a result of the checked boxes in the Places and Layers panel. If you want to remove something from the viewer, scroll through the panels and open folders to determine which boxes are checked and uncheck them.

- Experimentation is the best way to gain proficiency in Google Earth. Don't worry – if you want to quickly delete an unwanted placemark that you've created, just right click the title of the place in your Places panel and select Cut.

APPENDIX
Find It Quick: The "How To" Index

How to:

GMAIL - Chapter 7
Label:	*Add A Label To An Email* - 60	
Spam:	*Remove Spam Forever* - 66	
Spam:	*Remove Spam From Your Inbox* - 66	
Theme:	*Add A Theme To Gmail* - 67	

GOOGLE ALERTS - Chapter 6
Create:	*Set Up a Google Alert* – 53
Edit:	*Edit a Google Alert* - 56
Feed:	*Add a Google Alert Feed to Another Feed Aggregator* - 55
Gadget:	*Add a Google Alert Gadget to Your iGoogle Home Page* – 55

GOOGLE EARTH - Chapters 13 – 18
BLM:	*Search the BLM website* - 176
Download:	*Download and Install Google Earth* - 131
Folders:	*Create Surname Folders* – 154
Folders:	*Delete Files or Folders* – 155
Icon:	*Add a Photo to a Life Event Icon* - 196
Icon:	*Add Life Event Icons to the Map* - 196
Image:	*Copy an Image from Google Earth* - 157
Image:	*Save an Image* - 156
Land Patent:	*Plot An Ancestor's Land Patent* - 179
Maps:	*Find Plat Maps Online* - 170
Overlay:	*Create Your Own Historic Map Overlay* - 169
Overlay:	*Save Your First Map Overlay to Your Computer* - 171
Path:	*Add a Path* - 197
Placemark:	*Add a photo to a Placemark* - 141
Placemark:	*Add an Image to a Placemark* - 183
Placemark:	*Create and Name a Placemark* - 153
Placemarks:	*Move Placemarks Between Folders* – 155
Placemark:	*Rename a Placemark* - 185
Placemark:	*Revise a Placemark* - 185
Placemark:	*Virtually Visit and Mark the "Old Homestead"* - 181
Polygon:	*Outline the Area of Focus* - 189
Save:	*Save a location in the Places Panel* – 140
Tour:	*Create a Family History Tour Map Folder* - 195
Tour:	*Create a Virtual Tour Placemark* - 191
Tour:	*Record a Family History Map Tour* - 198
Tour:	*Record a Family History Tour* - 190
Tour:	*Save A Family History Tour Map* - 197
Tour:	*Save Your Family History Tour Map* - 193

www.GenealogyGems.com

Video: *Add Existing Video to a Google Earth Map* - 188
Video: *Add Video to a Placemark* - 186

IGOOGLE - Chapter 8
Create: *Create Version 1.0 of Your iGoogle Page* - 70
Gadgets: *Add a Gadget for a Blog Without the +Google Button* - 79
Gadgets: *Add Genealogy Blog and Podcast Gadgets* - 77
Gadgets: *Add Genealogy Gadgets* - 73
Gadgets: *Delete Gadgets You Don't Want* - 72
Gadgets: *Edit a Google Gadget* - 80
Gadgets: *Minimize/Maximize a Gadget* - 82
Homepage: *Make iGoogle Your Homepage on Internet Explorer* - 72
Homepage: *Make iGoogle Your Homepage on Safari* - 72
Layout: *Edit Your iGoogle Layout* - 80
Tabs: *Add a Tab to iGoogle* - 84
Theme: *Change Your iGoogle Homepage Theme* - 83

IMAGE SEARCH - Chapter 5
Retrieve: *Retrieve an Image That is No Longer Available* - 48
Search: *Search for an image with Google* - 41
Similar: *Do A Similar Images Search* - 49

SEARCH STRATEGIES - Chapter 3
URL: *Alter the URL Address to Find More* - 25
Webpage: *Take A Web Page Back To Its Roots* - 26

SITE SEARCH - Chapter 4
Website: *Search a Specific Website* - 36

TRANSLATE - Chapter 11
Detect: *Detect A Language* - 113
Document: *Translate a Document* - 112
Fun: *Convert Google Search to Pig Latin* - 117
Gadget: *Add the Google Translate Gadget to Your iGoogle Homepage* - 115
Text: *Translate Text* - 110
Translator: *Add Google Translator to Your Web Pages* - 114
Webpage: *Translate a Web Page* - 111

YOUTUBE - Chapter 12
Search: *Find similar content based on a found video* - 128
Upload: *Upload a video to YouTube* – 126

About the Author

Lisa Louise Cooke is the owner of *Genealogy Gems*, a genealogy and family history multi-media company. She is producer and host of the *Genealogy Gems Podcast*, the popular online genealogy audio show available at www.GenealogyGems.com, in iTunes, and through the free *Genealogy Gems* Toolbar. Her podcasts bring genealogy news, research strategies, expert interviews and inspiration to genealogists in 75 countries around the world.

Lisa is the author of a variety of multi-media materials including the *Genealogy Gems Premium* website subscription, her book *Genealogy Gems: Ultimate Research Strategies* (paperback, digital download, and for iPad), and the DVD series *Google Earth for Genealogy.*

In addition to *Genealogy Gems,* Lisa works closely with *Family Tree Magazine* as producer and host of the *Family Tree Magazine Podcast,* a regular article author for the magazine, and curriculum developer and instructor for Family Tree University.

Lisa's offerings are not limited to online. She is a sought after international genealogy speaker, and produces live presentations of *The Genealogy Gems Podcast* at top genealogy conferences.

Whether in person or online, Lisa strives to dig through the myriad of genealogy news, questions and resources and deliver the gems that can unlock each listeners own family history treasure trove!

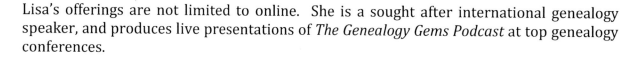